EVOLVE YOUR LIFE

RETHINK YOUR BIGGEST PICTURE THROUGH CONSCIOUS EVOLUTION

I0202904

BY SHEILA CASH

"Your future wants to speak through you. Let it."

Cover Design: John Matthews

Interior Design: Heidi Miller

Editing: Grace Kerina

Author's photo courtesy of Sheila Cash

DEDICATION

I dedicate this book to...

my mother, Shirley, who was never afraid to ask Why?;

to my father, Jim, who loved learning and was
fascinated by life;

to my brothers, Andy, Doug, and Jason, who
made every day and every inquiry incomparably
fun and memorable;

and to my kids, Amanda, Max, and Alanna, who have
given me the opportunity to learn so much about what
is really important in love and life.

Each of you have been my inspiration. I love you all.

TABLE OF CONTENTS

INTRODUCTION

As I danced around my soul's purpose for years — really, for a lifetime — the universe brought to me people I needed and who needed me. Each of them uniquely influenced my perceptions of life, which ultimately resulted in this book.

I was fortunate to have both a mother and a father who were seekers of knowledge. They were known to enjoy lively conversations that plumbed the depths of whatever subject was at hand. Through the years, my mother's way of exploring the world has been through open-ended questions. My brothers and I were raised to be inquisitive about how life worked and why things were the way they were. Group debates often rang out at home; they always turned into uproarious, witty, and priceless one-upmanships of comical insights. We left no stones unturned, speculating on everything under the sun, both existential and rational. I've retained that curiosity and passion about the world throughout my life and, consequently, so have my kids. Now adults, they each have beautifully expanded perspectives on life.

When I was a preschooler, I was in a serious car accident, sustaining injuries that put me into a body cast and traction for many months. During my long stay in the hospital, my grandfather died. I had been very close to him and he'd visited me often while I was in the hospital. That was my first experience with the death of a loved one, and I asked my mom many questions about what was actually happening to him in his state of what they were calling "death."

When I got home from the hospital, I recuperated on a bed that was positioned under large windows overlooking a regal oak tree outside. I watched the tree's leaves change with the seasons, falling away that winter to leave stark, bare branches behind. I asked my mom why the tree had died, assuming it had met the same fate my grandfather had. She explained that the oak was dormant for a while and that the leaves would return. I asked her over and over about the differences between the oak and my grandfather, struggling to understand why the tree would return to lush splendor in the spring but my grandfather would not. I continued watching and waiting for the elusive buds Mom promised would appear. Sure enough, eventually, specks of light green popped into view on the branches and the leaves unfolded day by day into full glory.

That is my earliest memory of trying to comprehend life and death. It was the beginning of what would become a life-long adventure of seeking any and all fascinating insights there are to be known about this universe.

Later on in my life, I became aware of interesting patterns regarding the people I knew. Though I never sought to be a counselor as I was growing up, friends and peers regularly came to me for support and solutions about whatever they were going through. That pattern began in my school years, when I spent time with schoolmates while on the playgrounds, and it has continued ever since.

I always considered those interactions to just be the way it was with regular friendships. When I have been asked to offer insights about a situation, my default position has leaned toward there not being *right* answers but rather perceptions that were practical in the moment. For whatever reason, many who were hurting and even suicidal came to me. In serious situations, I have always referred the person in crisis on to professionals who are better qualified to address them.

I haven't sought out, nor do I necessarily want to be in, the role of counselor, but I keep finding myself in that role. In some cases, old friends and acquaintances I hadn't talked to in years, even decades, contacted me to talk about their circumstances. Often, they say they simply wanted to share their words and thoughts with someone they trusted.

Some years ago, a woman I had only met briefly in a meeting contacted me to tell me of her suicidal state of mind. I had only spoken with her for a few minutes before that call, but she chose me to share her serious condition with. I gave her some spiritual support and then referred her on to someone more qualified to help her, but I then realized that the incident was showing me a lifelong pattern of one of my purposes in this life.

Another pattern that emerged is that I've often been asked to officiate wedding ceremonies. I am not a wedding officiant and never intended to get a license to become one. The couples I've conducted ceremonies for were already married legally and had filed their paperwork a few days before I conducted their ceremony. It is ironic that I view marriage as being an outdated institution in many ways —

I have no desire to be married again myself — and yet, in every case, the couples who asked have known of my personal feelings about marriage — but they asked me to lead their celebration anyway. I have been, and continue to be, happy and honored to conduct ceremonies for those who do want to be married.

Through those kinds of patterns, I've recognized and come to trust the authenticity that shows up in my life. You have such patterns, too, which you can discern if you reflect on your life and open to recognizing what they are. How the world sees us and treats us is one of the ways the universe may tell us who we are and what our purpose is. In this co-creative process, we can also make conscious choices and have the opportunity to show the world who we choose to be as well.

Those patterns of spiritual mentoring carried on while I raised three kids. I began to study expanding consciousness. I took courses on many different styles of meditation, sensory and psychic development, energy management, and sound healing techniques. I formed numerous groups for spiritual discussion salons. For 15 years, I studied with leaders in the fields of spirituality and consciousness and developed daily practices to deepen my skills.

As has happened throughout my life, people began asking me to teach them what I knew. I gradually started to form classes, groups, and workshops. Those led, eventually, to a weekly teleconference practicum with participants from all over the globe. My teachings have turned into more than 50 different courses on topics across the entire spectrum of spirituality, extra-sensory development, and expanding consciousness.

During that same period, I also studied the evolution of consciousness, taking interactive courses, and participating in active online communities with Craig Hamilton, Barbara Marx Hubbard, Ken Wilber, and others.

I have combined the knowledge and experience I've gained from those explorations in various related fields into a comprehensive online course experience. You can find out more about it at www.sheilacash.com

* * *

Over the years, in the midst of carrying on as an active soccer mom, I explored many world religions, from Unitarianism and Buddhism to Spiritualism and Hinduism. I was raised in a fundamentalist Christian home and my parents' backgrounds derived from the Church of Christ and Seventh Day Adventist traditions. After I married a Jewish man, I participated very actively in his extended family's holiday celebrations, and I attended temple on occasion.

I honor many aspects of each of the religious and spiritual traditions I've explored, yet I have discovered that, overall, I'm not much for labels regarding religion and spirituality — or even politics. Certainly, labels can bring understanding about tenets, history, and one's mission in life, but few people I've known have fit perfectly into a pre-conceived set of dictated religious or political components. I've witnessed various neuroses arise in some people who've tried to fit consummately into a social structure that didn't fit their authentic spiritual consciousness.

In matters of law, disagreements with the legal system should be taken up in court. In matters of spirituality, each of us chooses how much to conform and how much of our genuine feelings we can compromise on, and whether we will make excuses, justifications, and rationalizations for aspects of religious structures we may not be in harmony with, in order to stay among the flock.

My observation is that utter conformance in non-legal matters is an outdated paradigm and not realistic in this age of conscious evolution, with a globally integrating society on the rise. I've maintained and honor my own code of ethics, morals, and truths and continue to inquire deeply into life so as not to be tempted into hypocrisy.

Over the years, insights and revelations have come to me during meditations and while walking, driving, or dreaming. For a couple of decades, I didn't have time or space to write and so I would jot down perceptions on sticky notes, and then, eventually, with the advent of email, I would write notes as emails and send them to myself. Over all the years of doing all of that, I never got around to looking back at the notes I'd collected and had never considered turning them into a book.

Then, one day, I had a V-8 moment and realized there certainly must be a book within my stockpile of notes. Several more years went by until, with the encouragement of private students and friends, I spent some months gathering some of my collected notes together. A friend remarked that she envisioned my book project looking like a snow globe, with me standing in the middle and sticky notes flying around everywhere!

One of my longtime private mentoring students, Wendy Leon, offered to get the project rolling by gathering and collating my notes from years back. I will always be grateful to her for doing so, and thereby kick-starting this book. Ultimately, Wendy and I gathered and keyed into the computer more than 70,000 words of my notes. I stopped there, leaving the rest for another time.

This book is the culmination of those notes.

The words within this book are in no way seeking to be authoritative. They are ideas, insights, and theories to be considered and explored by you, the reader. By presenting them, I hope to open up some areas of awareness and offer food for thought. I hope some of your ingrained beliefs will be illuminated and brought further into your consciousness. I hope some fears will be quelled through realization of the rationales presented here.

May you realize what truth is for *you*. May you gain a compelling awareness of your authenticity and purpose. And may you feel intrinsically supported by the universe.

I invite you to open to the perceptions within — within this book and within yourself.

Sheila Cash, September 2015

CHAPTER 1

EVOLVING THROUGH AWARENESS

OPENING UP TO LIFE'S MYSTERIES

Somewhere, deep inside, do you question things about the universe that you've been told all your life? Perhaps you've become immune to ancient mythology, and karma in your personal life doesn't seem to make sense. After all, you really are conscientious — so why is life still so frustrating and unfulfilling?

You may feel gratitude for the legendary figures in history that suffered on your behalf, and still you wonder what place suffering has in the new consciousness you sense awaits you. You wonder about your genuine worthiness — on this physical plane and beyond. There are moments when you ask yourself, "Am I *really* good enough?"

You've been craving an authentic life for a long time now.

You may have been raised to have enthusiasm for the great outdoors, with an eye for the enticing mysteries hidden in uncultivated and uncontrolled nature. Perhaps you sought eye contact with wildlife, sought in their untamed gaze an awareness of hidden forces and insights into the ways of the universe.

You watched and learned from the clouds and weather patterns that came and went, then from the stars that formed celestial characters, and even from the circadian rhythms of the earth — cycles that began to illustrate hidden patterns that seemed to mean *something*.

And still, you sense that more is waiting to be discovered. You have a knowing that you've only scratched the surface of the great mysteries. You sense that the world holds even more consciousness than those theories, the ancient bodies of knowledge, and the myriad self-help books on your shelves have imparted. You feel that those theories are valuable up to a point but seem to be leading somewhere further...but where? You want to experience meaning and truth and purpose. You want to experience insights that resonate in your gut, without reservation. *But how?*

BIG QUESTIONS

Few among us have not asked ourselves big questions about life and the nature of the divine. At any point in your life, have you asked yourself any of these questions?

- How does God speak to me?

- What does God want from me?

- Why do I sometimes seem to be unheard?

- Why do some teachings I used to believe no longer resonate with me?

- What is *the truth*?

- What is holding me back?

- What am I afraid of?

- Why am I here?

What might happen if you looked, with an open mind, beyond those questions and the things you've been taught or told throughout your life to think and believe? What if you'd never been given answers to any of the questions above? What ideas or knowing might emerge from *within* you?

Many of us are told what to believe about the universe from the time we are born, rather than being encouraged to allow our own authentic insights and ideas to surface. We are told of ancient beliefs based in primitive thinking. We pick up prejudices, theories, and dogma about "the way it is" in current society. Maybe we've been fearful about opening to new ideas or acknowledging that openness with others. And yet we feel there's something more within us to be found.

A paradigm shift is needed now in order to align us with the expanded perspectives that are emerging as we humans rapidly and collectively evolve. It is time to open to greater freedom of thought.

In this book, I present a range of areas that may be useful for opening and testing new perspectives, with the aim of alignment — for you individually and for all of humanity collectively. Let's take a look at some of the concepts I'll be referring to in the coming chapters.

BIG CONCEPTS

Consciousness is the eyes and ears and heart of the universe. Our senses are a physical means humanity uses to awaken itself, to explore and grow into its fullest potential. Everything you see, hear, and feel informs the collective consciousness.

Conscious evolution refers to humanity's ability to guide our species into the future through choice. We can consciously make choices through co-operation and co-creation — or through the modes of separateness and competition. Every choice matters. *Your* choices matter.

The *evolutionary impulse* is the original, intelligent energy that took physical form and began evolving throughout time. It is the leading edge of evolution. It is the inherent inspiration that moves you forward in your life.

Evolution progresses through universal consciousness, which handles the trajectory of the sum of experiences of all unique aspects in a manner that is infinitely interactive. We humans have access to collective consciousness in this same way. All that has been learned and realized by others gets stored and is available for "download" by sentient beings. This is why ancient peoples on various continents around the planet evolved in similar ways at similar times over the millennia. The brilliant ideas that you come up with happen because you stand on the shoulders of others who've had their own realizations as they stood on the shoulders of others.

An *evolutionary* is a term used as a noun (rather than an adjective) within conscious evolution circles. It has come to mean a person who understands the importance of evolution at cultural and social levels. They have an awareness of the powerful and significant effects individuals have on our collective transformation. Evolutionaries seek creative and cooperative solutions.

Barbara Marx Hubbard, who has been referred to as "the voice for conscious evolution" has said, "We are the first species on this Earth who is conscious of evolution, conscious that we are affecting our own evolution by everything that we do, conscious ultimately that we ARE evolution becoming self-aware. Evolution by chance is becoming evolution by choice."

"...we align ourselves with the evolutionary impulse. You actually have to work against the evolutionary impulse in order not to grow. Unfortunately, many of us do."

– *Eckhart Tolle*

FREEDOM OF INQUIRY

In many areas of our world, we have evolved, culturally, to support freedom of speech. Although we all have the freedom to seek within our own minds and hearts *if we allow,* we may not live in a country or culture where we are able to speak our minds or express the knowings from our hearts. However, it is through sharing our questions, insights, and revelations that we come to better understand ourselves, our world, and our place in it. Further, we serve consciousness itself by inquiring and exploring. It is our universal birthright to ask questions like, "What lies ahead?" "What's out there?" Even more importantly, "What's evolving *inside*?" Not doing so squanders our birthrights and our gifts.

Inward and outward journeys equally evolve consciousness. It takes spiritual courage to ask big questions and to face what you find. We expand both our individual and collective genius when we more widely support exploration outside the confines of others' expectations.

This book gathers many "big question" subject areas into one place in order to present possibilities about how it all works together on our behalf — and what it means in practical terms for our lives.

HOW TO USE THIS BOOK

Although humanity has gained compelling and valuable knowledge throughout the millennia, we have never stopped

— and probably will never cease — our search for ever greater understanding. This is part of what moves us forward and keeps us inspired. Our curiosity is evolutionarily based for good reason. Hopefully, this book will make you think, and perhaps it will arouse those parts of you that want more ideas. The journey of exploration into the evolution of human consciousness presented in this book is not about pronouncing answers. It's more about opening our minds and hearts to expanded thinking.

My personal spiritual philosophy includes an integral view of the universe. My conception of reality contains no single answer but is influenced by and integrated with perceptions from our collective past, present, and the perceived future. I know that our common understanding is in a constant state of transformation. Though I explain my current perspectives, I do not and never will promote my views as final answers, because I do not believe in such a concept. My work is never meant to convince or convert, but simply to start conversations, to open doors of thought.

Step-by-step tools and techniques can be antithetical to an organic exploration. This book is not a step-by-step guide on how to awaken, because our spiritual growth takes leaps and dives, sometimes bouncing, sometimes careening along curving paths. The concepts presented here, however, can be instrumental in helping you clear out what's not serving you anymore, thus allowing you to lay a foundation for grounding and guiding yourself into your most authentic way of being. My experiences on both sides of mentoring have taught me that no matter what information or format is presented, each of us will pick and choose what is needed and what works for us at the place we currently are in our lives. Let your reading of this book, then, be an intuitive and personal process for you.

Questions and ideas are listed periodically throughout the book for your personal reflection. Take from them the insights that resonate with you. Use the blank pages provided to answer the questions candidly and openly, without editing or censoring yourself. If emotions such as anger or fear emerge, you may want to sit with your feelings for a while and journal about why you may be experiencing resistance. Ask yourself about the place inside you that is being touched? Which concepts, ideas, and questions strike deeper notes with you?

Answering the reflection questions gives you an opportunity to delve into yourself and your life meaningfully, through a broader context: to discern the aspects of your consciousness that are no longer serving you; to uncover roles you are meant to embody at this time; to move closer to your true authenticity; to discover what spiritual courage and responsibility can do for you; and to gain an expanded perspective on your universal purpose.

The better we know ourselves, the clearer the choices in our lives become. Moment to moment, we often become fixated on the little picture — on what's happening in this moment, what our reactions are, what feelings are taking over. Looking at the universal perspective can bring us much strength, empowerment, and comfort. Understanding our collective evolutionary path can bring genuine alignment to our individual lives. When we are aligned in this way, the door to love opens, and joy and peace emerge naturally. Vision and wisdom become ever-increasing parts of our lives.

This book is written for those of you who seek broader ideas about truth and purpose. It is for those of you who thirst for meaning that resonates in your soul. It is for those of you who want to lose your fear of the unknown. You will benefit the most if you are open to broader answers to the bigger questions and are ready to be inspired to leap beyond cultural norms and beliefs. If you can allow your mind and your heart to open, then these words are for you.

Here's to a renewed discovery of the vast magnificence that becomes you.

CHAPTER 2

EVOLVING OUT OF OLD CONDITIONING

GAINING PERSPECTIVE ON STALE STORIES

"Back in the day, we got up at 3 a.m. to slop the pigs and do our chores before hitting the five mile trail to school — come sleet, drought, and hail as big as bull's eyes...." I stood in line at my local bank behind a man who was telling his tale to no one in particular. He was just telling it; maybe to the bank teller who was otherwise engaged on the computer, maybe to me, or even just to himself...I couldn't be quite sure. What I was more certain of was that he had undoubtedly heard a similar tale from his parents when he was young, who had likely heard that tale from their parents. "Telled my kids, the good lord ain't got no worth for able-bodied souls who wanna lay in the sack sawin' logs all day. Ya gotta get out and saw real logs in the real world!" The old man was disheveled, wisps of hair flying out north, west, and east of his head. Thick canvas wrinkles from collar to shoes implied that he did indeed work from dawn to dusk, and probably beyond that. Maybe he had no kids to tell it to anymore — but he was still deeply attached to his story and likely would be for life. What I also couldn't help but notice was a pride — no, a bit more like righteousness — in the distinct tone of his voice, as though we should *all* get up at 3 a.m., and not a minute after. As if that was *the* standard for virtue.

As I stood there, I recalled another conversation with a friend who relayed that he worked from dawn to dusk every weekend on his yard, even repeating tasks over and over, though they had been completed already. His father had always told him that idleness is worthlessness. My friend just couldn't allow himself to rest peacefully. His parents had been dead for decades, and still he was exhausted.

Ah, the way of evolution. Learn through the lessons of others. Follow suit. Don't leave the flock. Be fruitful and multiply. Work your fingers to the bone. Ensure your ticket through the pearly gates. At least that was the paradigm of consciousness until recently. But the times, they are a-changin'!

Our old conditioned beliefs viscerally permeate the details of our daily lives. They show up as suffocating limitations in our decision-making and in our choices to do our authentic work in the world, to partner with the types of people we truly belong with, and in expressing our original thoughts, feelings and art. They can result in old paradigm states of consciousness such as martyrdom, victimhood, anger, worthlessness and many others that disempower us.

On your journey to an authentic and purposeful life, this early stage — that of clearing the outdated programming in your mind and body — is critical to an understanding of your self and the choices you make that will shape your life. This stage is fundamental to all others because until the *purposeless* is unloaded, attempts to reach the pinnacle of your authentic purpose will be made in vain.

Have you ever felt like you just don't understand life, or your place in it? Like quicksand, old beliefs may hold you in place or even seem to suck you under as you try to move forward in your life.

Your predispositions even affect what value you put on yourself as a human being. Taking a deeper look at how surreptitious programming affects your life, your love and your capacity for true fulfillment can bring you positive, life-changing insights.

Questions for Reflection

- What old stories still lurk in the back of your mind that could be fueling the emotions and actions of your life? Examples of conditioned stories are those that contain feelings of being victimized, feelings of worthlessness, feeling that others are out to get you, etc. Be open and honest with yourself.

- What adverse effects on your life can you identify that have come from living with those beliefs that are not serving you? Be sure to not make excuses for the stories as you consider their effects.

NOTES

NOTES

NOTES

FISH TALES

"What can we gain by sailing to the moon if we are not able to cross the abyss that separates us from ourselves?"

Thomas Merton

These days, we understand that the abyss separating us from ourselves contains a vast, ancient library of tales — notions passed on to us in order to teach us lessons, help us determine right from wrong, instill hope, and anchor our acceptance into heavenly realms in another dimension. This abyss was created out of brotherhood, faith, and love. Its stories were born from a need to understand a mysterious world through relatively primitive minds.

From roots of consciousness, we are each born into physical bodies and a multi-dimensional existence. We've been doing our best to rise to the occasion ever since. Ideas about the universe, our worth and value, and what is "good" and "bad" have been forming throughout our history, arising from our culture's beliefs and desires at any given time. Traditionally, a focus on survival necessitated an ego-centered approach to understanding the world.

We humans will always quest to explore the world, and our theories will always be primitive when looked at within the context of future standards. In this current age, we have the capacity to look back in history through the filter of our contemporary understanding and recalibrate our collective consciousness as we evolve forward. This gives us the ability to discern what is still useful and what is no longer useful to both our individual and collective paths.

Jean Gebser, a 20th Century philosopher, named a series of stages of consciousness that have occurred during our human evolution that include "magical" and "mythical" stages, among others. For a long time in our evolution, we needed a "magical" consciousness. We're still thrilled and delighted to watch a magician's tricks.

Sparks of the mysterious rise up in us when we witness an astonishing outcome with no comprehension of how it happened. The evolutionary part of us is impassioned by the enigma. Magic is fun. It opens us up to wonderment that there is more to be discovered. We are beings who seek answers — and will resort to making some up, if none are apparent. *Many of our current beliefs were formed in this stage of consciousness.* Without this inherent catalyst to seek, we might have ended up as mushrooms — staking out a supporting, nurturing environment and feeding off of it in place forever.

But, as human evolution will have it, eventually, we grow up. There's no Never-Never Land of eternal immaturity programmed into our world of unfolding existence. What is useful in one stage of our development is assimilated into the next stage so that what is *not* useful can eventually be transcended.

Early on, some of the mythical views relieved us of taking responsibility for our inner caveman. For example, in days gone by, if we humans killed in the name of God, it was considered not only the *right* thing but the *righteous* thing. At times, we were even awarded the promise of eternal life for it. At one time, we believed that gods needed to be appeased with human sacrifice. Variations of these beliefs remain embedded in some cultures around the globe. Ancient rationalizations such as these are not only outdated but critically dangerous to humanity now. Terrorism abounds. It's time for us to move out of archaic mindsets that keep our understanding of each other and the world stagnant.

WEIRD SCIENCE

Dr. Bruce Lipton is a rock star in the world of cellular biology and the relationship between our beliefs and the inner workings of our cells. His books serve as evolutionary stepping stones for our species at this time.

I met Dr. Lipton at a small, local venue early on, during his first book tour, and became even more inspired by his work and the awakenings it would produce for human consciousness. I related the importance of his findings to my own journey of excavating obsolete programming.

Clearly, my tastes had changed from the days of hanging backstage with Gene Simmons and Paul Stanley in the 1970s! Since the 1990s, I had been deep into intuitive work on the energetic roots of my own beliefs and uncovered fascinating insights into many of the choices I had made in my life up to that point. As decisions in my life became increasingly complex, for instance, over the course of an extended divorce process while raising three children, I had unearthed conditioned tendencies toward sacrifice and martyrdom.

Learning that the very cells of our bodies store old programming, that directs our lives subconsciously, explained so much about my state of consciousness and how it was directing my life. A journey of uncovering my own ancient operating system led me to empowered choices and actions. That process ultimately freed me to pursue my greatest authenticity — which was valuable beyond anything I had previously imagined.

You have the capacity to do this too, to reach beyond what you know, to find the un-programmed you, the unburdened you.

Deep meditations into the primitive roots of troubling and misaligned areas of your life are capable of revealing patterns of behavior that are rooted in the past and no longer apply to your current life situations. From there, you can consciously create a habit to change your beliefs.

Awareness is the key.

RETHINKING OLD MODELS
OF CONDITIONING

There are countless areas of outdated conditioning in contemporary society. Let's look at commitment as an example.

In centuries past, commitment in marriage meant that two people pledged to stay together "'til death do us part" and to be loyal partners for life. Statistics on infidelity and divorce are wide-ranging and dynamic, but we see that divorce is common and infidelity is even more common. What is evident is that many people are only committed until... they're not. At present, most of us in the free world can get divorced anytime. Legal and cultural support for couples to stay together has diminished dramatically over the last half century. So what is the point of commitment overall? Is the concept of marriage becoming antiquated in modern society?

If we look at our anthropological history overall, we see that we are not a species capable of foolproof vows. Yet we go on pretending that we are. Of course, some people do remain dedicated, fulfilling their religious and cultural commitments, and some percentage of couples are wedded until death. Love on its own can be unconditional and eternal. This is not to say we shouldn't attempt to bring order and steadfastness to our lives, but it is time to take a look at why we make commitments, and see if there is another way we can be together that aligns us more closely with our true capacities.

Consider this: *Commitment is an attempt to look for permanence in an impermanent world.* Our conditioning to seek permanence is misguided because the universe exists by an ever-changing flow. When we seek to indoctrinate ourselves in a way that is out of alignment with the universe, we eventually confront conflict.

In my practice of spiritual mentoring, I have seen many clients realize a great internal misalignment with the concept of commitment. *This misalignment doesn't mean we should not commit* — but rather that we need to be more honest with ourselves about our true capacities regarding permanence.

Questions for Reflection

- What do you consider to be the purpose of the commitments in your life?

- Does the reality of your commitments match your expectations about them?

- How might you reframe your understanding of your commitments so that you feel more aligned with them?

NOTES

NOTES

Another area of this type of conditioning is our tendency toward war. Peace is not yet the globally unified standard for conflict resolution. In addition, sacrifice is an act that is highly recognized and even decorated with prestigious medals. We have achieved unprecedented levels of independence in some areas of our world because of sacrifices people have made, but it can be helpful to step up to a more universal perspective and realize that we are still decorating people who kill people. Is there a relationship between sacrifice and the archaic consciousness of martyrdom in war? Are we as removed from the martyrdom of extremists as we think? How can peace arise from that level of consciousness?

The "us against them" mentality is also present in some political systems. In the U.S., a dominant two-party construct is set up to divide citizens *mainly* into one camp or the other. Though independent parties are gaining ground, they are not the majority yet. Increasingly, we no longer fit into such divisive lines. We tend to hold unique viewpoints on individual issues rather than adhering to whole platforms of ideology.

Historically, moving away from outmoded institutions and ways of thinking creates chaos and confusion during the transition period. But, over time, staying stuck in ideologies that no longer serve us results in even more stagnation and conflict.

Certain stages of consciousness are useful in each evolutionary period, serving a grand purpose, but only up to a point. As we evolve forward, we integrate all the knowledge that has gone before, assimilating more and more new information and developing new practices over time. We're meant to continue *building* on our current understandings, rather than staying in one place forever.

We are affected by old mindsets at a personal level, far beyond what we are conscious of regarding how we deal with others, how we make decisions and choices, and even how we feel about ourselves. Once you are aware of the energetics at play as a result of programming that is no longer needed, you can choose to filter your life through a consciousness that is more aligned with who and how you want to be in this world.

Questions for Reflection

- Where does an us-against-them mentality show up in your relationships and your work?

- For each instance, describe how this state of consciousness affects your beliefs about "them" and about yourself.

- How do those beliefs further separate and divide you?

- Reflect on the common ground that exists in each scenario and detail your thoughts and observations.

- What are your feelings about "them" now?

NOTES

NOTES

COMFORTABLY NUMB

Two types of collective conditioning many of us engage in by default are *denial* and *desensitization*. We're conditioned to accept that sales people may exaggerate the capacities of their products, that politicians' promises may never come to bear, and that job descriptions may not be all that accurate. We get used to an awful lot of "fudging" in our daily lives and become accustomed to not only considering it normal but even begin accepting it as our standard.

As children, many of us had a gut sense about people and situations that didn't match what we were being told about them. Over time, we came to distrust those feelings. We noticed as adults around us hushed up about alcoholism, abuse, and mental health conditions (among other things) and as they became conditioned into a state of denial. How can we lead lives of balanced discernment if we continue to build on ingrained fabrications?

Guilt and shame can throw us into denial as well. Even in the routine of our daily lives, there are many areas where our actions and our consciousness are not in sync. We cover up dysfunctional relationships, bad health habits, financial issues and more by stories of denial. Ethics around the foods we eat have gained much attention in recent years. More people are gaining awareness about the consciousness of animals as well as how they are treated in commercial farming. Jonathan Safran Foer wrote about his struggle to purge his consciousness while he was still eating animals. These poignant words he wrote had an impact on me: "...more important than reason in shaping habits are the stories we tell ourselves and one another. And I told a forgiving story about myself to myself." Foer's statement makes me feel his humanness and his attempt to keep himself comfortable *before* he stopped eating animals.

We all tell stories.

But we're only human. We try to protect ourselves and our loved ones. The world is so complicated that much of living is a stab in the dark, with uncertain outcomes. But because we're human, we keep trying. Aiming for a higher consciousness is really a stab in the dark too. Some of us are brave enough to eventually take that leap. Others disguise their humanness by denying and making excuses for actions that are not aligning with their knowing of a bigger picture.

The more aware we are, the harder it is to ignore what is the right action for our consciousness at that time. Foer's words illustrate the stage of limbo he was in during the important process of *reaching* for a higher consciousness. That's a stage that some of us spend a great deal of our lives in. There is much vulnerability there.

It is a worthwhile practice to simply *become more aware of your stories*, and to consider how your life is being directed in the midst of accepting life's red herrings without question. As you become more awakened, your choices in life will begin to naturally align with your most authentic life and purpose.

Questions for Reflection

- Do you remember any times when you denied your real feelings?

- What was the outcome of situations when you acted while being in a state of denial?

- What are the stories you tell yourself today about those particular situations and what happened?

NOTES

NOTES

NOTES

NOTES

NOTES

Desensitization is another form of old conditioning we succumb to. We are largely desensitized to many subjects in our lives: poverty, politics, abortions, domestic abuse, and ongoing prejudices to name only a few. We continue to be desensitized to certain issues, just as some parts of our culture were once desensitized to slavery. One early root of desensitization started in past millennia when people had no voice against their oppressors. They couldn't fight or they would be killed, and they couldn't flee because they needed the support of the family. In such situations, the brain freezes and ultimately begins to accept the offending person, ideology or environment in order to survive.

Today, many people deal with their work environments and their marriages by going into a state of desensitization. Sensibilities and intuition are turned off. Even logic often gets turned off. Acceptance turns to habit, and when desensitization becomes a habit, numbness sets in.

From an evolutionary perspective, desensitization creates the ultimate separateness between us. This is true between people, as well as between people and our natural environment. When we turn off our attention to a subject, little hope for any resolution remains.

Questions for Reflection

- What areas of your life might you be desensitized to right now?

- Do people tell you things about yourself that you have trouble believing are true?

- Do you ever notice that your loved ones seem to be desensitized?

- Could the areas in which your loved ones seem to be desensitized relate to your life in some way?

NOTES

NOTES

NOTES

ROCKS AND HARD PLACES

"Wanna fly, you've got to give up the shit that weighs you down."

Toni Morrison

Habitual reactions hold us in a status quo state that is based in the past. This is antithetical to a future created from a whole and balanced foundation. But changing your consciousness can be threatening to those around you. Often, others want you to stay the same so that they won't have to do any adjusting. They also may not be willing or able to face themselves or go deeper into exposing their own delusions.

We tend to mirror each other's deepest beliefs. As a species, we are still stuck in the tribal need to belong — which can keep us constrained collectively in certain beliefs or practices. If you move on, where does that leave me? And, thus, we go along with others who are just going along with others. We all keep each other stuck: they deem it desirable, so we buy in, we conform. In turn, they — whoever *they* are — remain empowered to keep deeming it — whatever it is — desirable. And on it goes.

We've spent so many centuries steeped in rationalizations, justifications, and denials based on cultural, tribal, and, ultimately egoistic reasoning that we don't necessarily know what's real and what isn't anymore. It is only when we get real with *ourselves* that the larger collective can follow suit and important changes can be made. Our creative selves are evolving. Changing times require changing solutions.

What if we talked more openly and often about our *real* feelings on topics we tend to be polite and agreeable about but that don't support our evolving consciousness? What if we found the courage to question the usefulness of our ingrained mindsets or practices on a regular basis? Do we have what it takes to face and accept our spiritual responsibility as *individuals* in order to evolve *humanity* to a level of greater clarity?

START IN THE NOW

The good news is we needn't clear out 100 percent of our old programming in order to be more balanced and whole. Let's leave the checklists and charts and start from where we are in this moment. Attunement to inner balance and being honest with ourselves will automatically release much of what's obsolete. The process of releasing is initiated by becoming aware of old beliefs as a natural part of our awakening to our future trajectory.

As you open up to your genuine alignment in the world, blocks and old assumptions will arise naturally to be recognized and noted. Welcome the blocks and the resistances you encounter, as they are *guideposts* to your most healed, integral self.

You aren't broken. You are where you are. This is how evolution has always worked. Your attention to, and recognition of, how and what you are thinking and feeling about yourself and the issues in your life will begin the process of releasing what no longer serves. The old ways will start to be replaced by the new ways as you choose to think and feel differently.

THE ONUS AND THE HONOR

We have the capacity to create our lives from an unburdened consciousness rather than having to be boxed in to the cultural limitations of the past. Our current generation will consciously process many of the myths, old beliefs, fears, and gunk from our collective ancient programming, because this is the first era to enjoy such widespread privilege of free thought and exchange of information. Unlike people in earlier eras, we now have access to alternative therapies, interest support groups, Internet connections and resources, and books that challenge taboos. The cultural revolution of the 1960s led us to a new stage of evolutionary development that continues to unfold.

Though we are left with the onus of purging dusty beliefs, we also have the honor of being able to consciously shape our new world by being fully present with what is true in the "now" moments. The purpose of evolution pushes us to process our beliefs emotionally, mentally, physically and spiritually on behalf of our ongoing collective future as a species together. Participation in this process is a gift of immeasurable consequence.

How will you choose to participate?

CHAPTER 3

EVOLVING DIVINE CONCEPTS

GAINING PERSPECTIVE ON TRANSCENDENTAL THEORIES

Before we go further into universal aspects of our lives, let's look at perceptions around divine beliefs. Many of us wonder if our beliefs are the "right" beliefs or if there is more information out there to consider. We often have questions. This chapter will give you the opportunity to review some ancient concepts and explore new ideas on theories you may have pondered.

KARMA

And they lived happily ever after.

Doesn't poetic justice feel satisfying? It makes you believe that all those who have done you wrong will meet their just end. You don't even need to handle it anymore. Just lie back with a fruity drink and let karma do all the dirty work for you. After all, they will only be getting what they deserve, right?

We love watching Cinderella passionately kiss her soul-mate after having been treated so badly by her evil step-sisters. We're gratified knowing that those repugnant pseudo-siblings will never find love because they've been so cruel. What goes around, comes around.

But what about the real-life mean girls you knew from high school who married well or became rich and famous? Do they deserve happiness? They were just so spiteful. And what about your sweet neighbor who served all those decades in the homeless shelters? She also went on church missions to teach the uneducated and gave her own resources so selflessly. She is still looking for love, isn't she? She deserves everything too, but is deeply sad in her declining health at this point. Oh, it must have been a past life sin then. Surely she was some version of Cruella de Vil way back when.

I've known abusive people who manipulated, cheated, lied, stole, committed illegal activities, smoked and drank all their lives — but were funny, charming and generous and still retained their family's love and their community's respect upon dying a natural death at an old age. What's up with that? Well, bad things happen to good people and good things happen to bad people. As long as we've had recorded history, we've been trying to figure out why.

I'm not setting out here to discuss the many variations on karmic theory, but to address the widely held theory that if one does good, one will reap goodness and if one does bad, one will reap negative consequences. It is also widely held that the degree of each action will match the degree of the result. In addition, some believe that a higher authority is judging each act and overseeing the consequence. Those who believe in karma tend to feel that the system is foolproof within the bigger picture.

For years, I've listened closely to my clients' needs to attach to stories of karmic rewards in this life or in the afterlife. They may not even use the word karma but the story around good and bad versus reward and punishment is always present.

So, why do we need this story?

Knowing that there is justice in the universe satiates our programming for equality in the world of good and bad, reward and punishment. Believing that the grave unfairnesses we've endured will be cleaned up in the afterlife, even if not here, makes us feel that at some level someone is looking out for us after all.

Questions for Reflection

- What is your belief about divine judgment?

- What do you believe about experiencing karmic retribution in this lifetime?

- How do you feel about the concept of receiving rewards and punishments in the afterlife?

NOTES

NOTES

So, what is happening in the natural world that handles this phenomena?

THE LAW OF CAUSE AND EFFECT

At the root of the concept of karma is a system of cause and effect, one of the natural laws of the universe. Cause and effect is a complex and dynamic organization containing an infinite number of catalysts and reactions, making karma not as simple an idea as "an eye for an eye." What is considered "good" or "bad" differs according to cultures, eras, and the egos involved. What's considered to be good locally for some may be bad globally for others. Widely held beliefs about karma imply that divine judgment is involved at some level.

But the universe does not judge us. We judge ourselves. So what is perceived as karma is simply the universe's attempt to balance in a homeostatic way. The universe is letting humanity work out its balance. This is evolution. Cause and effect leaves out the judge.

One of the ways we've dealt with our human need for justice is to set up our own systems of rewards and punishments. But our attachments to rewards and punishments have huge implications, particularly where war and peace are concerned.

Judgment and justice are nested in an early paradigm of consciousness where we sought to more clearly define our boundaries, ameliorate chaos, set forth a standard for growing civilizations and balance egos. *In this current era, might we be ready to outgrow a need for the fight between good and bad, reward and punishments, left and right, black and white?* History shows us that punishment begets punishment begets punishment. Egoistic reactions can never bring us to the peaceful balance we ultimately seek.

Forgiveness is an important step in the evolution of our egos. A barrier to forgiveness that some people experience is the feeling that if they forgive someone who has harmed them, the person forgiven will go on to live a carefree life, not having to "pay" for what they've done. Karma is a convenient remedy if the would-be forgiver believes that a higher power will exact revenge on their behalf. However, the *pure* act of forgiveness — forgiving without ego involvement — is the release of judgment and is, in itself, an attempt at balance. *If forgiveness is genuine, payback is not necessary.*

We evolve when we forgive with an intention of gaining understanding and being able to move on ourselves — not with an intention for revenge, karmic or otherwise. Forgiveness releases the hook of the ego. *Then the perceived balancing effect of karma is not needed. We have taken the responsibility to balance the situation inherently, through pure forgiveness alone.*

The natural law of cause and effect exists within our physical world and at the level of other dimensions that are close to the physical plane. The higher the level of consciousness, the more the extent of this law diminishes, as it is no longer needed.

Questions for Reflection

- Is anyone in your life waiting for your forgiveness? If so, describe the hook that is keeping them beholden to you?

- Do you feel that you need to be forgiven by anyone? How does that make you feel about yourself?

- What are your true feelings about revenge?

- What are both positive and negative feelings you would have about a life that contained no judgment of others or yourself?

NOTES

NOTES

NOTES

NOTES

NOTES

NOTES

Let's look at another theory humanity has linked to karma.

REINCARNATION

Closely related to karma are various beliefs about reincarnation. The commonly held belief about reincarnation is that the soul comes back after death to begin a new life in a new body. The notion of karma is the idea that transgressions from past lives can be "worked off" while encountering similar situations in the new life, by taking new actions from a higher consciousness. This pattern repeats in successive lives until the wrongdoing has been reversed by virtue. It is thought that individuals have lessons to learn and will keep coming back, life after life, until their learning has been sanctioned.

You may have experienced situations that seem customized just for you, to teach you "your" lessons. However, we actually choose, either consciously or subconsciously, to deal with particular issues in order to open the opportunity to ameliorate struggles and negative patterns in our lives. When you encounter situations you have chosen to process, they may seem to contain lessons about issues that originated before this lifetime, especially if the lessons keep coming back around.

Each of us has countless lessons to learn. At any given time, we can be oblivious to the many issues we could potentially recognize and confront. Many of us stay in dysfunctional and imbalanced patterns of behavior that go on for years, or even decades. But we can always decide when and how to change our perception and our actions. The more awareness we have, the greater impetus there is to shift. You have many opportunities to deal with people, places, and things; to choose when and how you learn what you learn. *The lessons you choose to actively recognize and process are based on your level of consciousness at any given time.*

If a change affects you deeply, you may be tempted to consider it *the* lesson of your life. However, there are many lessons that have the potential to change you and affect you deeply. Though lessons can feel uniquely designed for you, it is actually up to you to decide what your lessons will be. At any given time, you choose what mistakes you will learn from and overcome — or else avoid and turn away from.

Because we are each an integral part of the collective consciousness, on the whole we all learn from each other's processing of these lessons through the eons. What each of us experiences and, in turn, processes, spreads throughout the dimensions and into the collective consciousness, permeating all of humanity. The results of your participation are stored in consciousness for others to draw from. Your decisions and reactions thus inform and shape the course of human evolution as it moves forward.

Some people around the world have experiences of what they consider to be past life awareness, where they recall detailed facts about those lives. Because we are each intricately connected to the collective consciousness, we have access to the stored memories of all the lives that have ever been lived.

When children and others correctly recall memories of lives from decades or centuries past, they are effectively "downloading" those memories. Since we all derive from the collective consciousness, every life that has ever been lived is essentially a "past life" for every one of us. Some people are able to tap into collective consciousness and past life phenomena accurately.

The way to release "past life karma" is to face and deal with everything that comes your way to the best of your ability at the time. Because every thought you think and every action you take is stored in the collective consciousness and ultimately programmed into humanity's DNA, *the way you live your life is your distinct, invaluable contribution to humankind.*

When you have brought your highest consciousness to a lesson, and have dealt with it to the point where it is not charging your emotions but instead brings you a sense of peace and balance, you will no longer draw that particular lesson into your life. Moreover, you will know you have successfully processed it. This inter-dimensional education is how we learn from those who came before us and how we teach those who come after us. If we accept spiritual responsibility for ourselves, is there any need to hand off our actions to be judged by any being or divine concept other than ourselves? Is there any need for a do-over?

Questions for Reflection

- What have been the biggest lessons you've learned in your life so far?

- When was a time you consciously decided to learn a lesson?

- In your own life, how does the feeling of making a conscious decision to learn a lesson differ from the feeling of resisting that lesson?

NOTES

NOTES

NOTES

NOTES

NOTES

SACRED CONTRACTS

Another, related theory is that of *sacred contracts*, which states that your soul makes an agreement before you're born. Your soul's agreement contains a promise that you will discover your divine purpose and take actions toward it. A divine authority will guide you with clues and will bring you the people, places and things you need to fulfill your contract. Upon your birth, the contract is forgotten.

This belief of sacred contracts can provide purpose, but it can be limiting when misinterpreted as each of us having an *assigned* purpose. Actually, your purpose is of a higher nature than you could perceive. Believing you chose all the people and circumstances of your life before your birth may make sense, feel good, and give your life and circumstances purpose and meaning — but there's more to the story.

Believing that your lot in life is predestined is antithetical to evolutionary growth. The preordainment perspective is created from very close to the Earth plane, is ego-centered, and created for comfort. That level of thinking, including that theory, is our ego's need to control outcomes so vast that only the universe can manage them. A broader perspective allows more space for creation and personal empowerment.

You are born with a vast repertoire of skills, intuition and discernment with which to navigate your life. You have opportunities to create, learn, and evolve on behalf of yourself and humanity in boundless ways. The theory of sacred contracts is a popular notion that has sent many people on missions to find their divinely assigned purpose. While some people do feel a defined calling all their lives, many do not. Trying to zero in on *the* thing that is your mission in life can be futile — because as we mature and gain wisdom and experience in life, our capacity for fulfilling many purposes expands and evolves as well. You don't have only one purpose... so you can take a rest!

It can be empowering to understand that the circumstances of our lives are not preordained. Rather, we attract to us the circumstances that can use the gifts we brought in with us, to allow us to contribute, as well as cultivate, latent capacities. We are empowered creators. We process and create as part of creation itself, and this fuels evolution.

So, what is the soul's role within sacred contracts? Many traditions consider the soul to simply be the immortal quality of a living being. I believe that the soul is humanity's memory of itself in the universe, as remembered and expressed through the unique essence of each of us.

Your soul is the part of our universal consciousness you are uniquely tuned in to. It's the part you perceive because of the gifts you were born with. It's your angle and your piece of that gazillion-piece puzzle that makes up the evolution of consciousness.

Essentially, *you* are your sacred contract. Your gifts, insights, and even personality as you encounter the world — your unique filtering of life through your soul — evolves humanity forward. This is what is meant to be.

Next, let's consider one of the greatest divine concepts of all.

GODS

God means many different things to many different people. A god can represent security and safety, belonging, purpose, service and steadfastness. As an anchor and a creator, this divine authority is believed to provide guidance for all. Groups base their identities on their god's characteristics. Gods are given attributes of power and judgment. Some gods give unconditional acceptance, some give conditional acceptance. Throughout history, our attachments to our gods have been deemed worth warring over and killing each other over. The belief that we are beholden to a god drives us to worship, and also, in some cases, to project blame back onto the divine when things haven't gone well.

Some years back, a client of mine who found herself in financial straits asked, "Why has God forsaken me?" I asked her what she felt her responsibility in the matter was. After some deep thought, she realized she was actually disempowering herself by putting the culpability for her burdens outside of herself. Blaming has the ironic effect of keeping us *enslaved to the very thing we want to be done with* because we're not taking responsibility for dealing with it. We cannot blame divine authorities for our life's circumstances.

A belief that someone is watching over us puts us into a state of vulnerability. When we're at the mercy of a god, we are equally vulnerable to that god and to the world. In her TED talk, Brené Brown infers that vulnerability can open us to a sense of worthiness. Could the quest to obtain worthiness be what worship is about? Divine worthiness has been a mission for our species through the ages. Many people are now finding that taking on spiritual responsibility for themselves restores their sense of self-worth and empowerment. (We will be going much deeper into spiritual responsibility in a later chapter.)

Another customary belief about God and the archetype of the human form is that man is created in the image of God. If we look at the chronological history of God throughout past eras and cultures, what we can see is that God is created in the image of man. The tribal god who once was a vengeful, warring entity that sought retribution in blood has slowly matured into a more restrained and sensible deity, right along with large segments of humanity. As our egos have become slowly cultured through the millennia, so has the persona of God. I refer to this aspect of God as *eGod*:

ego + God = eGod

Consider the meaning of a God who continues to steadily correlate to our changing ego constructs over the centuries. Could we be projecting our collective needs and desires into a God concept ourselves in the present time, as individuals? *Has your honest, deeper perception of your God or universal authority changed as you have matured in life?* The way you answer this question has great implications for how you experience your connection with the divine and how you see yourself in the world.

Let's look at a couple of examples of natural universal phenomena that contain inherent characteristics of omnipotence.

THE EVOLUTIONARY IMPULSE

Many attributes used to describe God are also qualities of the evolutionary impulse. The evolutionary impulse is the energy and intelligence that burst out of nothingness to become the whole universe. That dynamic impulse imbues all of life. It is an intelligence that ultimately creates and supports every level of human experience, like many believe their god does. We create as we're being created. This co-creation fuels and informs our collective consciousness, which further governs our progression forward.

Ultimately, as vessels for this holistic process, our thoughts, actions and insights are inspired on behalf of this comprehensive entity. The comprehensive entity is the evolutionary impulse itself, not just the universe. We are the channels through which our collective consciousness processes all that involves humanity. *Every decision we make is immensely significant to the whole.* Indeed, as we make choices and then take action on them, we are doing so on behalf of all sentient beings and on behalf of the evolution of consciousness itself.

HOMEOSTASIS

What is the governing principle that makes all aspects of our physical world work together?

The key to life on this planet is *balance*. Balance is critical for the survival of life. The balancing act that takes place within our physical world is homeostasis. *Homeostasis* is a term that describes the survival of organisms contained in an ecosystem as well as the successful survival of cells inside an individual organism. Examples of homeostasis include the regulation of body temperature and the delicate balance between acidity and alkalinity in our bodies. The study of physics illustrates countless examples of the universe engaged in its balancing act. What we may be less aware of is the continual balancing that takes place emotionally and energetically.

Author George Leonard, who researched and coined the term "Human Potential Movement," discussed how homeostasis affects our behavior and who we are. One way Leonard illustrated the effects of homeostasis was by using the example of an unstable family. In this family, the father had been a raging alcoholic for years and then suddenly stopped; whereupon, the son started up a severe drug habit, which maintained the status quo of the family's previous dynamics.

I became aware of a similar, though less severe, phenomenon when a much-loved brother of mine passed away unexpectedly. He had been the family's default master planner for group activities. After he passed, I realized one day that I had taken on his role in the family. For decades, I had deferred to him. Then, without any conscious effort or awareness, I found myself stepping in to replace him in his family role, and thus restored that unique energetic balance to our family unit.

If we look to the ways of nature for guidance about how to be in this world, we see that homeostasis is the constant. The tenets of both moderation and integration are embedded within the phenomenon of homeostasis as well.

Our cumulative experiences through history have led us to believe that "moderation is the key." Aristotle, the Seven Sages of ancient Greece, and other notable figures have pronounced their own versions of advice about moderation. In my practice of spiritual mentoring, I've learned that harmony for the range of life's challenges can always be found through seeking moderation.

An integral view of life includes all perspectives. It isn't logical that the "All" or the "One" would take sides on any given issue. An integral view, with all angles being accounted for, is a balanced and whole perspective. The process of evolution itself will decide what stays and what goes. The evolutionary impulse works intimately with homeostasis as we seek to grow through exploration and creativity while maintaining this balance. As a species, we have learned through trial and error. We have evolved to possess an inherent deeper knowing around this overriding principle of homeostasis in the universe.

It is up to us to choose balance, particularly in response to perceived imbalances. Homeostasis is part of the evolutionary path of sustaining and promoting life. We are stewards for balance. Our highest spirituality includes navigating our singular and exclusive paths through this omnipotent and eternal principle.

We seek and seek for the best understanding of god. We argue, we defend, we kill over it. *But don't we really only want to be accepted, cherished, and protected?* Regardless of any particular tradition or beliefs...how much responsibility can we take on to accept, cherish and protect each other?

We embody deep inner quests for the right path to worthiness. But in the end, can a quest for divine perfection end up inadvertently creating a sense of unworthiness? Let us ask ourselves, "Is that quest empowering or disempowering? What will bring us the outcome that we are actually seeking from our souls?" Attaining compassion, charity, and love are universally agreed upon missions, *but can we incorporate morals and values in our lives for the inherent good they do us and our fellow humans, without being motivated by a fear of judgment?*

Whatever or whoever your god is, you are its tour guide for the world of form and the human condition. You are always connected to whatever you might consider to be the divine because ours is an integral universe. The concept of *god* represents your greatest potential. It is where you are evolving to.

You are in it. It is already in you.

Additional Questions for Reflection

- What types of lives from past eras have you resonated with?

- How does life in those eras fit or resonate with lessons you've gleaned in this lifetime?

- What characteristics does your god or omnipotent concept have?

- Describe feelings you've had in your life around support or betrayal from a divine authority.

- How do you feel about your worthiness and value?

- What are your beliefs about worthiness and whether or not it needs to be earned?

NOTES

NOTES

NOTES

NOTES

NOTES

NOTES

NOTES

NOTES

NOTES

CHAPTER 4

EVOLVING THROUGH INTEGRATION

GAINING PERSPECTIVE ON ONENESS VS. INDIVIDUALISM

Everywhere we look today, there is talk of moving toward "oneness" in contemporary spirituality. Indeed, the trajectory of our collective consciousness is pointing towards integration, not segregation. Back in the tribal era of evolution, we could keep up with the "one mind" easily because our exposure to life was localized and simplified in the form of the tribe. As a global society, however, there is much to assimilate regarding unifying consciously. Spiritual groups tout oneness as the epiphany of a consecrated state we should all be seeking. *So where does that leave our right to individualism and free thought? What is ego's purpose within the context of the oneness movement? Where is the evolution of consciousness leading us?*

HOLOGRAPHIC CONSCIOUSNESS

The rising climax of the Big Bang looks just like you. Yes, just like you! And me, he, and she. From potential, to gases, to galaxies, to matter, to biological life and consciousness, you have emerged as a sentient vessel of genius and creativity. Together, we carry the potential for all the greatest that life has to offer. We also bear the burden of processing the struggles that show up along the way.

Science continues to discover the characteristics of our holographic universe, of which our collective consciousness is a part. In a sense then, we live inside of each other. When my kids were young and seeking their separateness, as all well-adjusted adolescents and young adults will do, I teased them by reminding them, "Hey, you used to live inside of me!" We each started our life from inside another human. Though we can feel separate and autonomous at times in our lives, we remain connected through invisible threads of consciousness. In each moment, our thoughts blend with billions of others. Yet every solitary thought is utterly significant, contributing to and even changing the ever-dynamic trajectory of consciousness.

Each person, reflecting on each thought and acting for the highest good, in a sense, single-handedly takes the whole world forward. That is how meaningful you are to life itself.

MIRRORS

On your way to oneness, a valuable tool for understanding your life is to see people and circumstances as mirrors. You can ask yourself, "What is it about that person or situation that I resonate most with?" Also ask, "What about this experience feels negative within me?" The answers can be quite surprising. For example, you might identify someone in your workplace as egotistical and self-serving and even feel repulsed when near them. A common tendency is to say to yourself, "I'm not like that, so there is no mirror there for me!" However, the mirror may actually be that you feel taken advantage of and would like to have a more balanced workload like that person seems to have. The mirror can reflect areas where taking action on our own behalf will bring balance to our lives. *The more balanced we are, the less negativity we feel toward others.*

Another common mirror is that of "othering." We make the situation about "us versus them." We all know there is big business in war enterprising. But there are many common examples of waging war in our individual, daily lives, as well. A whole cottage industry has sprung up around criticism and slander. Every manner of denigration of others takes place on tabloid shows, certain talk shows, and even on comedy shows. What is the mirror around this? Are we fearful of being less-than? What is the price of being different? These character assassinations stem from cultural conditioning to uphold societal standards, even though those may not be authentic for the individual who is being belittled. This is an outdated mentality derived from a desire to eliminate any deviations from the accepted social norms. Staying in an "us versus them" consciousness obviously blocks the path to oneness.

We must always find the part of ourselves that contains the potential to be the problem we see; it's always within us, because we're human and we all contribute to, and we all derive from, our collective consciousness. One of the great values of mirroring is that it helps to assimilate our unique characteristics together with others' toward a consciousness of oneness.

Questions for Reflection

- As you think back on your life, what people or situations seem like they were mirrors for you?

- What spiritual lessons did they teach you?

- What mirrors are you currently looking into?

NOTES

NOTES

NOTES

NOTES

NOTES

NOTES

CONSENSUS

If we take the spiritual path to oneness, will everyone become the same?

In most societies today, it takes courage to *not* conform to commonly held beliefs, because in doing so you may be ostracized. In past eras, when our consciousness was focused mostly in physical forms, conformity was necessary — for example, for the tribe to overcome shared enemies with strength in numbers and accomplish other important tasks for survival. But we are experiencing a paradigm shift in consciousness, with tremendous expansion in human creativity, and conformity can impede our growth in many ways now. Allowing authentic creativity will advance the consciousness of both the individual and the collective. Without the change initiated by individuals stepping out of consensus, there is less progression forward. As the ancient poet Rumi said, "Conventional opinion is the ruin of our souls."

Evolving consciousness recognizes the contribution of individuals who break from consensus. Democracy is one illustration of this.

Although the valuing of diversity quells the complacency of the status quo, it should be noted that conformity itself brings collective synergy, which is also highly valuable, at least in certain situations. For example, humanity benefits immeasurably by putting minds together in scientific explorations and humanitarian efforts. In study groups I've led, co-meditation exercises have brought illuminating collective insights. Once again, both the individual and the collective have their function and place in the maturation of our conscious evolution.

Many people who are on a spiritual path focus on their consciousness of divine oneness. It can be more difficult to focus on spiritual oneness within our everyday physical forms, as opposed to oneness in consciousness. Omniscience is inherent in all things, including both the formless and what has taken form. However, when we give labels to that which is in form, such as male or female, Caucasian or Asian, Christian or Muslim, etc., those labels give us the false perception that our forms are separate.

Navigating a spiritual path is meaningful, but there is just as great a need to navigate a physical life well. Identifying with form is as important as identifying with divine consciousness while we're actually living our lives. This is where ego steps in.

SOME FACES OF EGO

Ego has gotten a bad rap lately, and we've all witnessed out-of-control egos. There is plenty of commentary about leaving ego at the door on the path to oneness. But is acknowledging ego only negative? Where does ego fit into evolutionary spirituality?

We are competitive beings. Any parent of a kid in sports will tell you about the early indoctrination of our precious young around competition. In this quest for excellence, low self-esteem and non-acceptance of self can be unwittingly planted and come to flourish. But the development of a better self does indeed take us further, faster, and higher. Ego imparts a perception of individuation, and it is this desire for uniqueness and excellence that inspires evolutionary movement out of stagnation.

Ego was formed, in part, so that the consciousness of creation could see itself with ever-fresh eyes in order to be able to create anew and expand. Ego drives our creativity as well as our quest for more, bigger, and better. The result is an amplified development of our physical, mental, emotional and spiritual capacities.

Conflicting egos and conflicts in general also inspire us. The impulse to find resolution gives us the drive to create better balance in the next moment. When chaos ensues, it means a rearrangement and rebalancing of energy is needed. This is one of the ways we transcend the old to evolve forward.

The struggles we endure and then process through during the most difficult times of our lives can lead us to places more desirable than we would have ever dreamed, had we not encountered those precise difficulties.

Questions for Reflection

- Consider the major times of conflict in your life. How did you get through them?

- What were the eventual results?

- If you had not experienced those particular conflicts, where might you be now on your path of understanding your life and your role in the universe?

NOTES

NOTES

NOTES

NOTES

NOTES

POWER AND CONTROL

The power and control issues we encounter within ourselves and in relation to others arise from ego as well. How do they affect the spiritual quest for oneness?

Some of us, especially those in the United States over a certain age, may have been raised "by the belt." Child-rearing routinely included Dad removing and using his belt to wield the power of authority to keep things in line. Until recent decades, corporal punishment was customarily allowed in schools in our society. Parental notification of such punishment may or may not have been conventionally included. Teachers, preachers, and neighbors often had implicit permission to discipline children in the community, since it was assumed that all "good" people were of the same mind on childrearing and civil obedience.

Fortunately now in the U.S., we've evolved away from that extreme power structure over children, for the most part. However, power and control issues remain present in contemporary society. Though our collective egos (what I call "WEgo") may well be evolving, a chain-of-command mentality remains in place in most governments around the globe. In the work environment, pay scales in the U.S. are still disproportionately in favor of males, as are positions of authority. Political candidates across the board promote more divisiveness than cooperation. Internationally, peace initiatives prevail but ego's quest for power still dominates relations within humanity.

HIERARCHIES

In some segments of society, the ancient paradigm of rigid hierarchies is slowly losing ground. Progressive young companies are gradually diffusing those structures and allowing much more autonomy for individuals. The privilege of working from home is commonplace. Democratic frameworks for designing and developing new products and initiatives have sprung up in the private sector. Brainstorming in groups is a popular technique for problem-solving within such organizations.

Seeking power and control creates a need for boundaries. While empathy does not exist in the state of separation, a state of oneness dissolves barriers. Research shows that whether we're developing our creativity or planning strategies, coming to a solid solution that works best for whole groups requires letting go of hierarchies. There is little room for them on the path to oneness.

Next, we'll look at one more way ego gets involved in the issue of integration.

CENSORING

Another traditional example of controlling by societal dominion is the practice of censorship. Governments and news organizations have habitually filtered information. Controlling information transfer in this way is an attempt to keep awareness from developing within society.

Expanded consciousness will bring a loss of power to the authorities in such places. Remaining as one mind keeps the status quo intact. *This is different from a spiritual state of oneness.* Censorship is an act of power by a controlling authority who is forcing adherence to one ideology or line of thought, whereas *a spiritual state of oneness consists of individuals who are coming to an blended, integral state of thought out of their personal choice.*

The advent of the Internet diminished the domination and prevalence of censorship. Although censoring still continues, much of the population now has or can obtain access to individuals around the planet in real time, at all times. We each have the ability to exchange views that are unfiltered and uncensored. We can explore free thought. The Internet is an inestimable tool for expanded consciousness. It has returned much power to the individual.

Next, we'll take a look at a comprehensive perspective for seeking the mindfulness of oneness.

INTEGRAL PERSPECTIVE

Much of life is organized around duality thinking: that which is considered to be right/wrong, black/white, conservative/liberal, good/evil, etc. When we polarize our feelings and beliefs this way, we miss out on the value of an integral understanding that brings much greater insight than any one myopic viewpoint.

The evolutionary impulse has blossomed into an infinite number of perspectives on any given subject. Beyond the land of *right* and *wrong*, there are countless ways to perceive. This gives us, as co-creators in consciousness, the leeway to explore and create boundlessly.

The great many languages, cultures, and environments on earth have given us the opportunity to know innumerable angles on human life and consciousness. Rather than having violent reactions to our differences, we can assimilate this understanding for an integral perspective on the human condition itself. *It is all the contrasting viewpoints simultaneously that get us closest to a picture of reality.* The universal perspective is never unbalanced or one-sided, but a well-rounded composite. This is the closest we can come to integrity, and therefore to oneness.

You are one tentacle of consciousness exploring the universe, filtering an infinitesimal slice of the *all* through yourself. *You are, nonetheless, just as essential as every other being.* We explore and process life together, and the cumulative result of our decisions moves humanity forward in existence. In this way, we live life through each other.

Therefore, we do not have to fully block other people's points of view. Given that there are countless ramifications for any perspective, *they* and *you* can't be fully right or fully wrong. Since each perspective is being created by a human, what you end up with is a view of the human condition in all its manifestations. If we were studied by an alien species, they wouldn't point at us and say, "Oh, those humans are right and the others are wrong." They might say, "Look at the diversity of behaviors within that species. See how some do it this way and some do it that way!"

COMPARTMENTALIZATION

Compartmentalizing is a way of deconstructing the integral perspective. It is a way we separate one part of our consciousness from another. When we compartmentalize, we seek to avoid the responsibilities and consequences of the areas we are shutting out of our awareness. This allows conflicting values and emotions to coexist by acknowledging them only one at a time.

An example of this would be a person who considers him- or herself to be devoutly religious, but who, while holding those views, also decides that a particular action counter to their religion's beliefs is justified, such as having an abortion. Another classic showcase for compartmentalizing behavior is engaging in adultery within a marriage. A spouse pursues and enjoys the company of another, then goes home and, without skipping a beat, returns to their role as husband or wife, without their spouse's knowledge of the affair.

This coping mechanism of compartmentalization can also be *helpful* in getting people through stressful periods they feel are otherwise unbearable. Soldiers are known to shut out their memories of the front lines of war while on leave with their families. People leave family dysfunction at home in order to get along in school and work.

Operating in this way can help individuals survive through certain challenging periods in their lives. But manifestations of compartmentalizing can carry over to become a way of life when unchecked. Black/white, good/bad, and right/wrong thinking — symptoms of compartmentalization — can infiltrate our entire lives and segregate us from other people, philosophies, and whole segments of life.

There are not only individuals coping with their own lives, but we have an entire species engaged in compartmentalizing areas of life experience. The result is racism, capital punishment, murder, oppression, and many other societal ills. The repercussions are monumental.

When we are able to contain all views together in harmony, we come closer to an enlightened state of oneness. Rather than choosing love or hate, we can accept that both love and hate *can* co-exist. We can blame and forgive at the same time. We can disagree and still appreciate. In doing so, we are more able to access the greatest range of the human experience.

And life is all the richer.

Questions for Reflection

- Remember a time when you allowed yourself to have your own point of view, even though it went against established views. What happened? What did you learn?

- Have religious or political ideologies influenced personal decisions in your life? If so, when and what happened?

- What areas of your life do you think you might be compartmentalizing today?

NOTES

NOTES

NOTES

NOTES

NOTES

It is commonly believed in spiritual circles that love was the first emotion of the universe. One of the deep meditations I lead takes the group on a journey in consciousness back to the Big Bang and then forward in time to our current lives. Along the way, we simply allow the emergence of every sensation and organic knowing. Each person speaks periodically, reflecting on their experience. The first time I led this meditation was on a global teleconference. What the group ultimately experienced together was the awareness of trust emerging as life began. We gleaned that trust is the impetus for the movement of each next step for life in evolution. Trust dissolves limitations to the creative process of being. Trust is love *blossoming*.

United we solidify, divided we diversify. Humans inherently seek both solidarity and autonomy. Both matter. Together, they harmonize in an integral movement toward oneness that is capable of boundless growth. You can choose to join others in their thoughts and beliefs or you can be a catalyst for new understanding and growth. Either way, your contribution to the state of oneness in consciousness will have an effect on our evolution.

CHAPTER 5

EVOLVING THROUGH TRUTH

GAINING PERSPECTIVE ON FACTS AND FALLACY

One day when I was a teenager, I walked along a beautiful park trail on a sunny fall day. I was rapt in contemplating life and the many issues that my teen years were confronting me with when it came to figuring out my path. Academic texts were teaching me their versions of what life was about, while ancient texts had their own renderings. The people in my life also had their own versions of the stories of their lives. Suddenly I had an epiphany that struck me profoundly, and has stayed with me ever since:

Everything is about perception.

Life wasn't about what one person thought versus what another person thought. *No one was right and no one was wrong.* This realization informed my mind, heart, and soul from then on. It has proven to be the most valuable filter for understanding the world that I have ever come across.

LIFE AS MAKE-BELIEVE

We make everything up.

We project how we think we're perceived in the world, what we're capable of, how worthy we are, how successful we can be, and what we deserve in our lives. We decide whether it is ok to kill animals and humans, in war or in utero, and whether or not it is deemed healthy to ingest alcohol and other substances. We make up ideas about what we consider to be good and bad, what punishments fit which crimes, and how many people should represent our personal interests in government. We project laws, medicinal remedies, and child-rearing philosophies. We made up the institution of marriage and defined what constitutes fidelity within the legal structure. We've constructed rules and regulations about how our children should be educated. We've devised major religious structures all over the planet.

We rationalize and justify beliefs to suit our desires. Scientists devise experiments to fit their hypotheses. Rigorous standards for experiments and testing are designed around a particular inquiry and then put into place. The inquiry itself directs and defines the outcome to varying degrees. It has been shown by quantum physics that we find what we're seeking.

Often, our beliefs are formed first, and then we marshal facts to fit the beliefs we already hold. Statistics can be used to present countless angles on the specific outcomes we want to illustrate. *Although studies bring us important insights that further our understanding of the world, the truths found within them will only remain until a more advanced under-standing replaces them.*

All of this influences how we evolve forward in consciousness.

The notable aspect of this observation is not whether any of these contrivances are valuable and purposeful for our species, but that they have been made up. None of our projections in any of these areas are absolute, as *absolute* is, ironically, a relative term based only on our current standards and understanding.

As we can see by a study of history, our understanding evolves as we evolve. All the valiant efforts and brilliant minds that have gone before have brought us to a foundation of security, organization, and innovation to keep us moving ahead in current times. They, too, made up their lives and their societies and theories. Through this cycle of creativity, we are able to advance from one step to the next.

Why do we make things up? *Because we have an inherent ability to choose the beliefs and structures that suit our purposes at any given time.* Because we have not yet evolved to a point in our collective consciousness where we are comfortable operating from a place of complete choice, and total autonomy is not practical for society, so we construct realities which suit our immediate state of consciousness. We build in limitations that seem to keep us safe and understanding the nature of reality — as it is, but not necessarily as it could be seen if we had more open minds.

If we didn't make things up, all would be mysterious. Mysteries at the core of existence make us uncomfortable. For many people, faith steps in to alleviate that particular discomfort. Are we at a point in our evolution where we can accept mysteries within the universe without feeling insecure? Are we ready to take a look at our beliefs around divine safety?

When viewed through a much deeper lens, even those tenets we traditionally thought were solid become more mysterious than ever. The good news is that this doesn't need to make us feel unsafe, because whether we're safe or not is also a concept we make up. We all know people who roll along through life with confidence. They feel safe in the world. We know people who carry paranoia and skepticism through their lives and are paralyzed by it. One manner of living is not actually safer than the other. Each perspective comes from accepting existing made-up stories and continuing to make up new personal stories to live by. What we believe about and create from our own stories influences our lives, our prejudices, our minds and our hearts.

Ultimately, we're living lives based on our stories.

Questions for Reflection

- What are some of the stories you've chosen to live by?

- How do those stories make you feel?

- What stories might take you closer to your authentic goals?

NOTES

NOTES

NOTES

NOTES

NOTES

MAJORITY RULES

At every point in our human history, we adopt certain beliefs to be *the truth*. We tend to settle on those truths as if they are the final answers. In traditional societies, once a truth is adopted, dissenting may bring harm to the individual. The status quo is considered a conventional stronghold to be defended. But that posture damages our ability to evolve consciously. *So-called truth is a moving target, shifting through the ages, because ours is an ever-changing universe.* And it always will be.

What is considered to be truth by humanity is simply what the majority or authorities believe at any given point in time.

Our current cultural conditioning has significant influence on what we presently accept to be true. We often accept by default the state of affairs that government officials and major news organizations report. We forget that we can question the biases of science and academia as they announce their current theories. We know paid interests skew information but we become numb to looking closer and confronting how.

In U.S. pop culture, reality shows are hugely popular. They purport to show what is happening in people's lives behind closed doors. We get caught up in the drama, forgetting or not knowing that such shows are largely constructed with intention to focus on specific issues or conflicts — scenes staged and heavily edited. This isn't to say that the population necessarily believes such shows to be genuine depictions of real life, but that we begin to become desensitized to what the truth of the average life looks like. Reality show viewers begin to imitate the characters they watch. This is an example of reality blending with fantasy, and the way we look to others' "realities" for guidance as we construct our own.

Questions for Reflection

- How much of your life is designed by you rather than by big business?

- How much do you look to others' realities — parents, organizations, celebrities — to create your own reality?

- Have you ever disagreed with a widely held opinion, whether of friends, politics, or religion? If so, what sort of feelings come up around that for you?

- What might happen if you allowed yourself to explore your own true beliefs at a deeper level?

NOTES

NOTES

NOTES

NOTES

EGO'S CONTRIBUTION

Egos bring personal contributions to the status quo of so-called truths. If we were all the same, we would tend to stagnate in smug complacency since we would "already have it all right." Fortunately, egos challenge the leading edge of ideas and creativity. Despite the accumulation of inevitably biased notions of truth, our different viewpoints are very important for producing a comprehensive awareness for the greater whole.

The evolutionary impulse gave us each the power of personal discernment to use on the countless angles that are available to us. You are not just a spectator. You are an important creator of your own path, a creature of cognizance. What you glean, intuit, understand, and realize is invaluable to humankind because as we expand individually, we expand collectively.

The challenge comes when we fight to assert our opinion as the *only* one. The ego can induce a desire for control — but knowledge cannot progress as long as the quest to control people, circumstances, formulas, and definitions is present. *The need for control is in inverse proportion to our capacity to obtain the purest knowledge possible.* An allowing mind encourages progress — which, unfortunately, large segments of the population fear. When the need or desire for control is in place, knowledge is driven out.

Commonly accepted and agreed upon standards in areas of knowledge can be significantly beneficial to our collective comprehension, but it is the deviation from those standards that is necessary for progression to occur.

QUESTIONS, NOT ANSWERS

As creatures of a higher consciousness, we have a mission to seek answers. We're uncomfortable without them. This is life's way of moving us forward. As a young person, however, I was far more interested in questions than answers. Answers felt too final, and very inhibiting. Answers could be boring but questions were exciting. The potential that existed before the questions were asked was even more intriguing.

We can come to understandings that satisfy us, but that does not mean those conclusions should be set in stone. If we can't come to an answer, we are often tempted to contrive one that will pass credibly. Answers can stagnate the quest and potentially disempower the seeker. Answers close doors that questions keep open. The more words brought in to answer a question, the harder it can be for knowledge and wisdom to emerge.

Perhaps it is time for us to mature out of the paradigm of needing to attach to answers, and at the same time learn to feel secure with embracing the open quest.

Questions for Reflection

- How do you feel when encountering questions that you do not have ready answers for?

- Do you have a fear of being wrong? What are you afraid will happen if you're wrong?

- What questions do you have about life and the universe?

NOTES

NOTES

NOTES

NOTES

MULTIDIMENSIONAL PERSPECTIVES

We perceive more than one dimension at a time. Physicists are developing theories on an expanded range of dimensions that exist. Truth in one dimension seems false if analyzed from another dimension.

Similarly, if you analyze something from the higher consciousness of the big picture, it will appear completely different than if viewed from an egoistic or personalized perspective. We've all heard the sage phrase "hindsight is 20/20." Looking back at memories often gives a very different perspective on what happened than we could discern when we were right in the middle of the situation.

We are most familiar with the natural laws of the universe as they operate within our three-dimensional perspective. Those laws may not apply in other dimensions and universes. Current studies at the quantum level of physics are turning previous theories on their heads. Our instruments for measuring and testing are not sophisticated enough yet to give us the highly advanced understanding we will eventually evolve into. We move ourselves toward a perpetual paradigm shift into new discoveries when we value other dimensional perspectives as credible alternative views.

Questions for Reflection

- Can you look with hindsight at situations in your life from a big picture perspective?

- Recall details about an event in your past that affected you deeply. How does your original perspective differ from your bigger picture perspective?

NOTES

NOTES

NOTES

NOTES

FLOW

Truth, like evolution, is never static. The familiar adage "it came to pass" implies that "it" did not come to stay. The nature of existence is change. It can't be any other way, or life would cease to exist. Our levels of awareness transform in tandem with the world around us.

Classic teachings often guide us into a fixed reference point on any given subject. Concrete definitions on explicit concepts make us feel, subconsciously, that we are sheltered from ignorance and are therefore more in control. We humans tend to have a need to be right, but "right" is difficult to keep pinned down if truth is always changing. Over time, much dogma and many details are built around original benchmarks of "right," and those eventually become much ado around an immobile precedent, rather than opening us up to a wider range of perspectives.

Truth can never be a stagnant point of thought. Even as we are in the midst of interpreting, the thing we are trying to interpret changes and evolves. The universe is in constant flow. The evolutionary impulse is imbedded in every quark of the universe — eternally observing, seeking, and shifting.

Confined thinking is anachronistic to our current evolution of consciousness. Adaptability of cognizance is what is needed to align us with the natural flow of the universe in its unfolding.

ALL THINGS ARE CONNECTED

There is always simultaneously more than one correct answer to any question. We can look through a lens of science, art, math, or philosophy on any given subject. Though these perspectives may provide contradictory information, none are unconditionally wrong. Each perspective has its own merits.

One of the exercises I lead my students through is assessing an issue using a bag of random items as a tool. In the bag are common items like those you'd find in most houses: a pen, a sock, a spoon, a candle, and dozens of other items. I ask students to reach into the bag, blindly pick out one item at a time, and relate it to an issue we're discussing. The pertinent and constructive perspectives each person arrives at are quite amazing. Great guidance is often obtained through this simple tool. Why is that? It is because no matter the questions being asked and no matter the nature of the tool being used, all things in the universe are related. When given the opportunity, our minds can "see" into the integral perspectives of the interconnected universe.

Years ago, during the discussion salons I hosted, I introduced the concept that two plus two does not necessarily equal four, when we go beyond the traditional math formulas we're familiar with. This declaration generally met with dissension, until we parsed through some examples using water.

Two buckets of water could be divided into a thousand parts, in which case, five hundred parts plus five hundred parts would equal one thousand: in this example, one (bucket) plus one (bucket) equals *one* thousand. Or the two buckets might instead be added together into a larger bucket: so, one plus one equals one. And on it goes for an infinite number of possible arrangements.

Although that particular illustration is simplistic, the understanding beneath the example can be transferred to every possible view in life: We need not attach to any one particular answer on any subject.

Our attachments are what result in thinking that there are no other answers in our personal lives, and give rise to thoughts like, "I don't fit in to the status quo," or even, "I'm not worthy." Forms of neurosis arise from limited thinking. *If you remember that there are always more options, then expanded opportunities will be available to you in every moment.*

In some way, every point, angle, or understanding contains some relevance to the integral picture.

ABSOLUTE

We tend to think that natural or universal laws are absolute, and yet quantum physics shows us that, even if that was true, we still don't know what the full context of an absolute *is* — within our relatively primitive understanding. In many fields of study, absolutes work very well in devising theories that take us to magnified insights. Everything inherently has a relevant aspect that is "true," and that is what we begin to work with. This simplifies some of the variables so that we are able to see the structure and relationships to other elements, leading us to greater conceptual understanding.

But logic is not the only way to explore. Whether or not there are eternal absolutes cannot be confirmed, because these are always subject to an ever-changing universe as well. Although we can recognize seemingly standardized patterns and principles when they are "slowed down" enough for us to discern by our current measurements, all things are relative — even the absolutes. In the bigger picture, absolutes may be simply the slowest-changing premises we humans are capable of recognizing. Even observations that are thought to be timeless and eternal can be updated.

Your own progress forward in consciousness will be well served when you learn to perceive in relative terms rather than *attaching* to a need for absolutes in religion, science, philosophy, or anything else. This will keep you open to ever newer, always updated insight and information. You will no longer need to cling to or defend your absolute positions. As your rigidly fixed postures dissolve, your life will flow more fluidly.

Questions for Reflection

- Do you have fixed beliefs that you can identify?

- What emotions come up for you when you consider optional views to those beliefs?

- Do you generally take the majority opinion to be truth?

- Where do the roots of your beliefs come from?

NOTES

NOTES

NOTES

NOTES

LETTING GO

A practice of letting go of what you think you know, and allowing all possibilities, will activate a broader palette of options for problem-solving in your life. When you feel a knowing in your heart and your gut about information that seems beneficial, honor it, be still with it, and revel in the further treasures now ready to be excavated.

Although truth takes on many forms, you don't need to memorize, absorb, or study all of them at all times. *You can take onboard aspects and perspectives that relate to you and your life and that lead you to either integrate the understanding you need or let go of that which no longer serves you.* We glean "truths" according to where we are in consciousness at any given time and what we need in order to take one step further down our unique path of purpose.

Enjoy the journey.

WHAT IS TRUTH?

Our truths are frequently based on wider, societally conditioned beliefs about right and wrong. They can keep us in straightjackets of consciousness, less aware of our ability to step outside of stagnant beliefs.

Any one perspective is inherently limited because it is only one perspective rather than a whole and integrated view. If truth is only perspective and all perspective is limited, then how *true* is truth?

Truth is subjective and collective. It is the sum of being able to perceive points from every angle. We will only ever be capable of attaining a fraction of this perspective. Truth is really just the leading edge of our understanding. It is nothing more than our story, individually and collectively.

Ultimately, truth is a myth.

* * *

So, what can we depend on? Is there no validity to rely on at all?

Yes, there is. Much of the information we deal with has enough validity for us in any given era to take us to a higher plane of understanding. *The objective is to not become righteous or mired in any staid point.* All bits of knowledge are valuable for certain people at certain times in certain situations. In each moment, there is a seed of veracity that's useful for you. *As you quest for spiritual awareness, you can choose the aspect of truth that empowers you over the one that disempowers you.* What truth will move you forward toward what you seek?

What is the point of seeking truth at all?

We're programmed to increase our knowledge. We do this most effectively by integrating information we have while remaining open to all expanded possibilities and permutations. We want to feel confident and competent in the world. Wisdom results from putting all the fragments of available information together into an integral composite.

You can change the beliefs you've attached to as *truth*, if you desire. My practice involves helping people change their stories when they've come to feel that the ones they've lived by are disempowering. Embracing the full concept of truth with heightened discernment will set you free from standards that no longer serve you and from limitations that hold you back.

CHAPTER 6

EVOLVING THROUGH MATURITY

GAINING PERSPECTIVE ON SPIRITUAL COURAGE AND RESPONSIBILITY

"Maturity doesn't advance linearly, like you steadily and readily becoming more profound in your thinking. No, it staggers and stumbles like a drunk."

Jarod Kintz

Maturity is generally defined as the ability to respond to life appropriately through experience, and with purpose. The status of maturity is distinguished by independence of thought and non-reliance on guardianship.

Due to the Internet, in today's society we can interact globally without the intervention of authority. We're being intimately exposed to reclusive beliefs and lifestyles that we never knew existed and therefore, have had no experience with. We have the opportunity to act with fewer and fewer limits. In the past, we sat in the same classrooms with the same textbooks that our parents had used, in some cases, and we had access to little more than an *Encyclopedia Britannica* that had been published years before. Uncensored, cutting-edge information was very difficult to come by.

The old moral codes of the past cannot keep up with our worldwide exchange of information and our instant engagement with each other in today's world. Social media expands the edges of socially acceptable behavior. The need for personal responsibility is greater now than ever before.

Spiritual maturity includes cultivating the courage to be self-determining in aligning your own authentic beliefs and conduct with your highest consciousness. Spiritual clarity comes from resolving to be fearless in recognizing hypocrisy, contradictions, separation, and myth for what they are.

Awareness in these areas brings cohesion to the integrity of your consciousness.

COURAGE

Fear is a driving force within us. It wakes us up, makes us pay attention. It reveals, it challenges, it changes us. Fear gives us the opportunity to be brave.

We need a lot of courage in our lives. From taking our first steps to taking our last breaths, there is much we do alone and for the first time. True courage could not be cultivated without the presence of fear. How we handle fearful circumstances determines how we see ourselves and how we see the world.

We all have wounds from the past. Few of us have escaped trauma, whether emotional, physical, or mental in nature. In some cases, wounding was not inflicted intentionally but rather as an effect of others' attempts to get through their own struggles. In any case, the aftermath still leaves casualties behind and the result is the same in terms of how those situations create pain and fear.

Fear can reign supreme. We can be scared of being unloved or scared of being ostracized or scared of losing our way. Some people are secretly scared of eternal damnation, and of not knowing the real nature of the spiritual realms. We feel inferior and worry that we don't have the right answers, as so many of us have looked "out there" for truth and alignment.

PROJECTIONS

Our projections are a manifestation of living our lives externally rather than internally.

While we look outside of ourselves for answers to our questions, we have a tendency to also look around out there for someone else to blame. Crediting others as being better than we are or, conversely blaming others for faults of theirs or of our own, reflects a fear of trusting ourselves. *Both of these projections disempower us.* We fear that we aren't capable of acquiring the best answers. If we blame, our fear is about not being capable of owning our actions. When we gratuitously put others in charge of our lives, we become disconnected to our own authenticity.

Although our problems can create fear, they can also allow us to escape our fears by distracting us from them. If your problems are big enough and loud enough, they draw your focus to the myriad details around those issues and away from your inner awareness — where the answers actually are. Staying in fear can keep you in a small place, where you won't have to step outside your comfort zone. In that place, you won't have to face potential failure. When you stay in fear, you give yourself and your power away. We have given our power away to spouses, parents, bosses, friends, and political platforms. With awareness, we can take it back.

A traditional way we have relinquished responsibility en masse was by creating a symbolic receptacle of all that we don't want to deal with, and then giving it horns, a forked tongue, and red-hot skin. This is a misguided attempt to adequately anchor and justify our separation from ourselves. Ironically, this only further victimizes us.

Handing off our burdens rather than facing them with courage causes more powerlessness. Those who feel powerless may seek desperately for power in other areas of their lives and end up bullying, stealing, raping, or killing to get it. Fearful reactions to powerlessness abound.

SPIRITUAL BULLYING

In my youth, there was a lot of spiritual bullying that went on around my town. Verbal righteousness thrived in our community, though the actions taken relating to those words were not always as saintly as the words themselves. As a sensitive child, I felt the agitation that was projected in people's God-fearing dialect. Mixed messages about punishment and reward, both here and in the hereafter, overflowed from pulpits and porches. As I grew older, I began questing to find peace and meaning as an antidote to that duplicitous backdrop of my childhood.

FANATICISM

Fanaticism is a dangerous state of consciousness. The belief that one way of being should be accepted by all people is a delusional condition. The familiar adage, "He doth protest too much," is a recognition of more going on beneath the surface. We have been culturally conditioned to the point that some percentage of us considers authoritative rhetoric to be legitimate rather than the bullying it really is. The paradigm of thinking in terms of black or white, left wing versus right wing, and good and evil precepts contributes to the vicious cycle of violence, and war and death. Instability is born from fearful, extreme thinking. Take it a bit further and you end up with terrorism.

FAITH

Many people rely on faith to provide courage. I have known people who were well served by faith throughout their lives. Others I've known used faith in a way that inadvertently disempowered them. As their struggles became more and more injurious to their lives, their allegiance to the tenets of their faith kept them from doing the processing necessary to understand and overcome their issues.

Faith brings hope and security. But facing adversity and taking courageous action in one's life is what brings authentic confidence and the skills needed to forge ahead through life's difficulties and make it out the other side.

Faith can disguise a need for courage, because all power has been handed over to a divine authority. Strong faith overcomes the feeling of being vulnerable to fate. But when we are faced with difficulties, a true embodiment of courage comes from the willingness to step forward into our natural-born gifts.

Similarly, the need to be "saved" stems from the magical and mythical stages of human consciousness and indicates a reluctance to be spiritually responsible for oneself. A need to be "saved" also creates a false sense of subordination and reflects a need for both approval and protection.

Supplication is in our DNA, and we've been conditioned to feel naked and afraid without it. Some people fear *not* believing the handed-down stories from past millennia. We humans also have a great fear of being ostracized.

Rising up to personal enlightenment that is not divinely (or socially) sanctioned has been deemed evil and even psychotic at certain periods in our history when it was considered sacred to stay small and, thereby, remain blessed and protected. Digressing from the norm can leave us feeling vulnerable, but only if we believe that must be the outcome.

If we allow ourselves to digress from the norms in our quest for spiritual enlightenment, we can nonetheless follow the common tenets of charity, brotherhood, and compassion on behalf of our own honor, and on behalf of all those we share the planet with. In doing so, we may aspire to a high level of responsibility regarding those qualities, without fear of being judged from beyond. A paradigm shift of thinking, feeling, and understanding our power helps us begin to create our own outcomes — among which are lives lived with honor and spiritual courage.

It is not sacred to stay small. Silencing your self and limiting your thoughts is antithetical to conscious evolution. It's time to rediscover our voices, our authenticity, and our personal empowerment — with integrity and respect.

We need courage from within as well as from the outside — from society or the god/s we believe in. We need to risk being wrong, and accept the vulnerability of speaking our truths. We need courage to step forward into our inherent gifts and into our authenticity. We need courage to allow others to be different from ourselves. We need courage to define both internal and external successes for ourselves. We need courage to stand in the conviction of intuitive knowing, to feel secure, and to know that we are only human. We need courage to face the fear of death. We need courage to love.

Let's allow ourselves to develop spiritual courage for the gifts of comfort and inspiration, hopefulness and optimism. This will carry us forward in evolution in the highest vibrational way.

Questions for Reflection

- What place does spiritual courage have in your life?

- Do you feel inherently safe and protected?

NOTES

NOTES

RESPONSIBILITY

"Sometimes I want to ask God why he allows famine, poverty and injustice in the world when he could do something about it, but then I'm afraid he might just ask me the same question."

–Anonymous

Responsibility and accountability are the main points behind most codes of conduct, yet our creative minds find countless ways and means to absolve us of these traits. Past traumas, hormones, pointing-the-finger, and all manner of excuses are tools for avoiding the call of duty. Indeed, research in the field of holistic medicine cites a great range of illnesses that are subconsciously manifested by this kind of avoidance.

We have ample documentation of humanity to be able to look back and see the far-spreading consequences of our actions throughout history. Let's look at a few barriers to responsibility.

IMMATURITY

Violence is a spiritually immature way of getting what we want. It is an advanced and dangerous adult version of preschoolers' developmental phase of growth where they experiment with hitting one another and grabbing the toy away. Spiritually immature adults shoot, maim, rape, and kill to grab land, titles, and power. Global talks on peace temporarily appease parents and international boards. But we hear military authorities talk strategies before the violence, and then after the violence, give us reasons to justify the violence, and then talk to the public to commend and honor those who committed legal violence on our behalf. As long as those in power remain spiritually immature, we will continue to seek peace through war, just as some seek divine accolades through terrorism.

Spiritually, some of us have remained in that preschooler mentality. As we mature in consciousness, we will be able to further evolve peace and heal the human condition in life-giving ways. Every person may not be ready for this — for instance, those who still think violence is the answer to violence. But just because not everyone is ready, doesn't mean those of us who *are* ready shouldn't go there at all. We must start somewhere. Those who understand cooperation and harmony will lead us forward.

Voltaire said, "No snowflake in an avalanche ever feels responsible." Assuming responsibility for our own thoughts is of paramount importance. The larger systems in which we are embedded are slow to change, but we can still maintain and foster reverence for the understandings that keep us out of chaos and use them as a mirror.

We can't fix it "out there" until we fix it "in here."

HOLDING ON

Processing through and letting go of unresolved pain aids in being able to progress into a future that is whole and free from past imbalances. *The decision to let go of that which holds you back needs to be a conscious one.*

Ultimately, the quality of your life is based on the choices you make. Not on what your parents did, what you endured in past relationships, the economy, the weather, your job, or your age. You and only you are responsible for every single choice you make. No one else is going to process your stuff. No one else is going to live your life for you.

We can't evolve forward if we're holding on to beliefs and choices from the past that no longer serve us.

Let's stop trying to make others accountable for our own conditions.

DEPENDENCE

We commonly depend on others to act on our behalf. Someone else will call 911. Someone else knows CPR. Somebody will surely blow the whistle. We've become adept at handing off perceived liabilities.

If we don't have enough autonomy to be responsible for ourselves, then we may also be malleable from outside influences, such as segregation, bigotry, and even advertising to tell us what to look like, how to act, and what we should be wanting in our lives. We lose our sensibilities when we're steeped in a consciousness of dependence. We lose our empowerment.

When we take spiritual responsibility of our own volition, we give power to our higher consciousness, to the most reverent part of ourselves: our reverence for life, for the planet, for animals, for kindness and brotherhood. Let our empowerment stem from unity and love.

A POSITIVE PURSUIT

While there are states of consciousness to let go of on the path to spiritual responsibility, there are also areas to cultivate. One of these is the pursuit of happiness. If you want happiness, it is your responsibility to choose it.

The United States' Declaration of Independence avowed the right to pursue happiness. But while the state can provide conditions for the *pursuit* of happiness, it is each person's spiritual responsibility to actually create and allow that happiness for themselves. This is a pertinent example of a need to be accountable for one's own condition. Happiness is a process that happens within. Any attempts to blame outside ourselves is an excuse to separate oneself from happiness or, in other words, to create suffering. It is up to each of us to choose and then find our own way to happiness, alignment, and fulfillment.

Questions for Reflection

- What are your obstacles to taking personal responsibility?

- If you haven't already, what would it be like to consciously make a choice to pursue happiness?

- What areas of your life might change completely if you made that choice?

NOTES

NOTES

NOTES

NOTES

NOTES

Spiritual maturity is not for the fainthearted. It requires determination and perseverance. It's about the capacity to expand. *It's about the ability to find lessons in your hardships that will serve others.* The evolutionary impulse is beckoning you to transform.

The reward for attaining spiritual maturity is having the opportunity to use our gifts to be a "way-shower" to others. We can consider being strong, compassionate, and able to see the big picture to be a reward in and of itself. Our journeys are about making peace with humanity and with our own human condition. Let's aspire to spiritual maturity and move toward a more peaceful, creative, and loving future together.

CHAPTER 7

EVOLVING THROUGH AUTHENTICITY

GAINING PERSPECTIVE ON THE UNIVERSAL PLAN

Well, who are you? Who, who, who, who? I really wanna know...

Pete Townshend for The Who

Millions listened to those lyrics on long-play albums in the 1970s during a continuing cultural revolution that upheld existentialism as a legitimate inquiry. Imbedded within the song's questions is an age-old quest to know who others *really* are. What are their true intentions? What do they want from the world? What are they really made of? Knowing others also sheds light on who *we* genuinely are.

We ask the question "Who are you?" because so often people wear disguises. People are camouflaged by their clothes, jobs, accents and the choices they make. Most are not even aware of their own charades as they blend into the pageantry of their lives, falling into roles that may have been naively devised by parents, broader authorities, or their own innocent accord. Mostly, we passively succumb to the culture around us. In the process, we can lose track of the origins of our most authentic selves.

The evolutionary impulse seeks to emerge through your unique take on the world. You bring what no other on earth can bring to the bigger picture. "Who are you?" This question echoes through human history. Listen closely, as this is your calling from the evolutionary impulse itself, made to lead your individual free will into the grand design of evolution.

A NEW MODEL OF SUCCESS

Early on in my adult life, while my peers were barreling forward to make their successes in the commercial world, I was most drawn to making success in my inner world. That is where real fulfillment happened for me. At the time, I didn't have a name for what I sought, but I now know to call it *authenticity*.

Through my years of spiritually mentoring others, I witnessed that those who sought authenticity were able to come into true harmony and well-being, while those who remained attached to the constructs of their outer lives were less able to realize inner peace. There is a growing paradigm shift in our culture from outer success to inner success, and *authenticity* is the word for this new model.

Questions for Reflection

- What are some roles you've taken on in your life?

- How were you aligned or misaligned with each role?

NOTES

NOTES

NOTES

NOTES

PERFECTION IS NOT NECESSARY

Choosing to travel the path of your authentic self does not mean your idea of perfection must be attained. The universe does not expect supremacy from you. Everyday sainthood has been a somewhat subconscious mission for some people I've known who were raised in religious environments that supported such an ideology.

There is a paradox in having an expectation to embody the mind and heart of a saint while knowing that you will never be ordained as such. The human condition of which we are all a part did not end its apex with the essence of Mother Teresa. Nor was it arrested with the rise and fall of Saddam Hussein. The characteristics of humanity range from Mother Teresa to Saddam Hussein and encompass everything in between and further beyond. No matter where you fall on that spectrum, you are only human.

Being aware of what is not authentic in our lives is as important as recognizing what is. Start where you are. Some of us can barely get through some days. On other days, we're able let go of something that previously held us back. On still other days, we may glean some insight that changes our lives for the better. The path may be tangled, but along the way we learn and come to great understandings that lead us to our next steps. We do this by being who we are, rather than trying to be someone that we're not.

PRETENDING

"Few are those who see with their own eyes and feel with their own hearts."

Albert Einstein

When we spend years of our lives pretending to be someone we're not or doing work we're not aligned with, it makes our authenticity difficult to perceive. Boris Pasternak said, "Your health is bound to be affected if, day after day, you say the opposite of what you feel, if you grovel before what you dislike and rejoice at what brings you nothing but misfortune. Our nervous system isn't just a fiction; it's part of our physical body, and our soul exists in space, and is inside us, like teeth in our mouth. It can't be forever violated with impunity."

Our brains are programmed to repress or shut down if we can't fight or flee. Maybe your boss is unbearable. Maybe you can't fight your boss without losing your job, and you can't flee because you don't have time to look for another job that's better, and you're not in a position to take a cut in pay, and going to a competitor would ruin your reputation in the field. In such situations, our sensibilities can turn off. Logic can shut down. As we accept what we must accept (stuck in this job for now), the original repression (unbearable boss) is forgotten and our focus shifts to survival. Whether logic shuts down about our situations at work, in a marriage, or in the community, the resulting *misalignment* makes us detach from our genuine desires.

The energy expended in pretending to be someone you're not, and holding back who you really are, can cause dysfunctional patterns and health conditions that might otherwise be avoided. Mind-body research and related health studies expose the critical function of *authenticity for health* in our species.

Fortunately, in many countries, our current options for realigning are broader than they used to be. As Danielle LaPorte says, "Leave the flock." The flock uses sameness for safety. But at this point, individuals have evolved great capacities for expanding in consciousness and advancing human fulfillment in ways the flock is generally not up to.

Personal transformation and world transformation are struggling to grow within a species that is generally only adapting to its larger environment little by little. Shedding the sheep's mentality of deciding who you should be based on the flock's expectations is a step toward excavating the roots of your own special creative force in the world. You will begin to align with new relationships that speak to your heart and mind when you look inside for the answers to the question, "Who am I?"

The pressure to stay safely with the flock shows up in all sorts of societal expectations. Cultural images and ideas of beauty and monetary success bombard us. When we put on masks and disguises in order to conform socially, we lose track of our natural and organic essence. You may have experienced feeling as though you just don't fit in, and wondered why. We've been conditioned to believe that we must conform, but we understand more and more these days that uniqueness is actually a gift and not a curse. The individual's authenticity may just be beyond the bounds of a stagnant status quo.

Some people have made tragic choices over whether to leave their flocks and how to do that. We've witnessed a trend of LGBT suicides with adolescents and young adults over not being able to face society or accept themselves within an environment where they face rejection. Perhaps the latest ruling on same-sex marriages will help to reverse this trend.

In the transgender community, Caitlin Jenner has spoken about both the exhilaration and the peace that her transformation has brought. Some of her adult children have spoken publicly about how much happier and more engaged she is, and how her alignment with her true nature is bringing peace to family members who are open to her new identity.

Individuals who have the courage to transform their own lives are on the leading edge of the evolutionary impulse's quest for authenticity.

Questions for Reflection

- In what ways have you felt pressure to be "perfect"?

- When and how have you pretended to be someone other than who you know you are?

- Have you ever left a relationship, group, or larger organization because you felt misaligned with them?

- Who do you want to impress or please in your life? How does what they want for you differ from what you want for yourself?

NOTES

NOTES

NOTES

NOTES

NOTES

NOTES

AUTHENTIC SOULMATES

Who hasn't dreamt of getting snugly with the person who is destined to be *the one and only...* a person seemingly made just for you?

The key to ensuring your very own happy-ever-after lies in your honesty with yourself. Your unique soulmate can't possibly come to you if you are putting on airs with your own self in the mirror each day, let alone with the people around you. Your task is to be as much of your natural self as you can be.

The key to finding your soulmate is giving potential partners the opportunity to witness the depths of your genuine desires, preferences, and dreams. After all, those are what you and your soulmate will be aligning with through the years to come. If you're not honest now, there can't be authentic alignment in a future together.

So many of us put on a charming but false song and dance routine in the beginning — the one we think the other person wants when we're first developing a relationship. Although that time-honored technique is highly effective for luring a partner, the engaging theatrics rarely last long. When the smoke has cleared, your potential partner may say, "Where's the person I thought I knew?" When you cater to the other person in a relationship, and your behavior derives from a place within yourself that is not authentic, the apparent alignment within the relationship comes from your false self.

As we mature in relationships, we tend to grow into our more authentic selves. Then the two people who originally aligned the inauthentic versions of themselves so well, are now no longer in sync. At this point, it's common to hear blame: "You aren't the person I fell in love with." Now, the only way the relationship could make it is if you both remain as your false selves and stay in co-dependency. Or, conversely, if you attempt to move *together* toward greater authenticity and acceptance, you may still thrive in partnership. If one person in the relationship does allow authenticity to emerge, after the relationship has been established, the mutual alignment must recalibrate in order to remain viable. When *both* partners allow authenticity to emerge for themselves and for the other, they have a chance of staying on a trajectory for a fulfilling future ahead together.

To forge a long-lasting relationship with a kindred soulmate, bring your most authentic self to the beginning of the relationship. People who are genuinely attracted to your authentic self have the best chance of being keepers for the long haul. In turn, when you're attracted to your partner's most natural self, there's an authentic match.

It is important to note that once we engage in a relationship, we must give space for our partner to continue to grow into their *maturing* authenticity. We often want to hold partners in the space that we knew them in the beginning. But evolving consciously includes changing, and the more adaptable we are, and the more we honor our partner's authentic changes, the more fulfilling the relationship will be.

Relationships that blossom within authenticity from the beginning have the best chance of aligning over the long-term. No questions will emerge about why you ended up with that person in the first place. Relationships aren't just about snaring a spouse anymore. True love is giving your partner the freedom to be who they really are, not merely what you want them to be, and claiming the same treatment, expectation, and, indeed, birthright for yourself.

Questions for Reflection

- Describe a time when you pretended in order to develop a relationship?

- Have you ever gotten to a point in a relationship where you felt that you no longer had any idea of who the other person was?

- How did the relationship turn out?

NOTES

NOTES

NOTES

NOTES

NOTES

MANY PATHS

There are a great many paths through life we could each align with if we so chose. Contemporary society rarely blinks an eye anymore at the person who has worked in several entirely different career fields. That would have been unheard of decades ago. The universe isn't persnickety about ensuring that your discoveries in life come in right on time according to some universal checklist of life development.

If you encounter apprehension about your path ahead, realize that it is likely not the path itself that is causing the fear — but the consequences or changes you may face in the present in order to get there. You can look inside and make a distinction between your feelings arising from your current situation in the moment and your feelings about the future. What's important is what you do with each moment. That's where you find the choices all along the way that will be "right" for you. *Every choice will be right if you pay attention to learning what each moment, person, and situation brings for helping you develop your own spiritual maturity.*

You can thank the voices of the past and the voices of your peers who have an opinion about what you should do — the voices of your mom and dad, the voices of guilt and perceived regret, the voices of lost jobs, lost loves, and the multitude of perceived mistakes. Thank them for being the mirrors that show you where your best path should be. And then resolve to let them go. They brought you understanding. Now you can move on.

As you move into greater authenticity, you may feel powerless at first, if you are accustomed to feeling powerful through your false self. Look for and try to recognize tendencies to weigh, measure, rank, and rate yourself — those are ego distractions. Remember that perfection is not the goal.

Although competition can inspire great new paths, there is no need to compete when you're going for your own authenticity through a focus on creating or inventing that which you are aligned with. As you create, give particular notice to what draws your attention and speaks to your heart, as these are callings from the evolutionary impulse, made to steer you according to the grand design of evolution.

Discover what is *not* you, identify what *is* you, and then be brave and make a choice about what you want. Ambivalence can become a comfort zone of its own. Begin choosing, and leave indecision behind. You cannot go wrong, as all possible choices are catalysts that take you deeply into the lessons of your life. *The point is to choose.* What good is a calling, if it's not heeded? Refining your individual preferences, choice by choice, creates the direction of your life. This is the pinnacle achieved by using your free will.

Questions for Reflection

- What do you yearn to create?

- What activity makes you lose a sense of time altogether?

- Have you changed your mind about what vocation you have wanted for yourself?

NOTES

NOTES

THE BIGGER PICTURE

Authenticity is the catalyst for a new era of evolution. Because life itself seeks balance through homeostasis, I believe our DNA at birth is inherently balanced for the bigger picture of evolution within our species. Every aspect of who you are begins in your DNA and remains calibrated, all your life, to your unique experiences and the direction the evolutionary impulse is seeking for the bigger picture. *Your authenticity was designed to balance our species for a specific collective trajectory forward.* Therefore, the more in alignment you are with your genuine essence, the more in the universal flow your life will be. It is when we are out of alignment (inauthenticity) that our physical, mental and spiritual faculties become unbalanced. The depths of your desires, creativity, insights, and capabilities are an integral part of the blueprint. *They are how you serve humanity.*

Perhaps the evolutionary impulse embedded a certain amount of resistance within us in order for us to not barrel forward unheeding. Conceivably, we needed to develop certain mindsets or characteristics before we "take off" in authenticity — characteristics like stability, reason, and peace. Manners, altruism, and cooperation are essential for getting along together in society. Safety and balance for all as we progress is imperative. We needed to mature within the constructs that keep us balanced in order for it to be possible for us to grow beyond them.

* * *

Spiritual engagement — realizing and accepting our own genuine beliefs, understandings, and truths — will bring evolution out of the "story ages" and move humanity toward greater actualization of the universal plan.

The evolutionary impulse is cheering for you, wanting you to succeed. When you are aligned, you will come alive in ways that you never dreamed of before. Choose to empower yourself. Live who you really are.

Relish being you.

"You already know who you are and that peace, that peace that we're after, lies somewhere beyond personality, beyond the perception of others, beyond invention and disguise, even beyond effort itself. You can join the game, fight the wars, play with form all you want, but to find real peace, you have to let the armor fall. Your need for acceptance can make you invisible in this world. Don't let anything stand in the way of the light that shines through this form. Risk being seen in all of your glory."

Jim Carrey

Additional Questions for Reflection

- What values or philosophies have you retained through your life that you may no longer align with?

- What areas in your life would you like to change?

- Who are you?

NOTES

NOTES

NOTES

NOTES

NOTES

NOTES

NOTES

NOTES

NOTES

NOTES

CHAPTER 8

EVOLVING THROUGH PURPOSE

GAINING PERSPECTIVE ON INDIVIDUAL, COLLECTIVE, AND UNIVERSAL PURPOSE

We humans look for purpose and meaning in life. We want to know why we're here and what life is all about. For a few lucky people, meaning and purpose are obvious — but for many, meaning and purpose remain obscure. Some people seek meaning through success, but find that outer success without a sense of inner meaning can be an empty experience. True happiness is temporary if not attached to meaning and purpose, and fulfillment comes to those of us who seek those qualities in our lives.

One of the greatest gifts of consciousness is being able to create meaning. This is one of our biggest privileges of being human and living life in physical form. We discover, create, and expand meaning *as* we live our lives.

MEANING

I've found meaning through extensive processing of the bounty of events of my life. What inspired me to continue processing through very difficult circumstances and issues was that *I had not yet found* meanings that made sense of those events at the time they occurred. It often takes being willing to let go of ego and rise to a universal perspective in order to see the why and how of many of the issues we encounter. My pattern has been to carry on until I am able to come to understandings that feel truly authentic. When I become aware of balance and peace, when I sense them in my bones, I am able to move on.

We expand meaning for ourselves through the actual processing we do along the way. Meaning is not a landing place. It's not static. It's not a destination. It is a dynamic, symbiotic process of realizing why we're here. Meaning and purpose feed each other in a collaborative and synergistic dance.

The evolutionary impulse organized itself so that it created consciousness on its own behalf, and then developed the capacity to coordinate the next steps, at every moment, in every place in the universe, and within all dimensions. This universal organization includes *you*. Your own individual consciousness creates meaning for you.

Sometimes people attach themselves to meaning that has been created collectively by the current culture or by a narrower group that they're associated with, such as a religious institution. When this happens, it is sometimes assumed that the meaning has been predetermined. *Whether that meaning is actually authentic for an individual person can only be determined by that person.* In other words, you get to decide for yourself what's meaningful to you.

The grand plan for humanity is based on the entire collective consciousness. I don't believe a master checklist is hiding in a dark hole awaiting completion. *Rather, the grand plan is the culmination of every part of consciousness in the entire universe working together.* Every sentient being contributes, and the evolutionary impulse coordinates each and every step along the way.

Questions for Reflection

- What meaning have you gleaned in your life?

- What differences can you feel into between the meanings of your outer, visible life and your inner desires and values?

- Which of the areas you've gained meaning from were introduced by institutions or organizations that you've been exposed to?

NOTES

NOTES

NOTES

NOTES

PROCESSING

Our collective purpose is to process all that comes into our lives — physically, emotionally, mentally, and spiritually. Each and every aspect of our lives comes to us to be uniquely filtered by our own particular consciousness. How we deal with circumstances, relationships, health, and every other choice creates the expansion of the leading edge of the universe.

While we often lament mistakes we've made, those mistakes actually bring us chances to *learn* what not to do. They help us know ourselves better and further refine our understanding of life. We learn from our own and others' misjudgments.

Conflicts in life are also useful mirrors for us. They show us where to shift our thinking and what needs to be harmonized with or transcended. Rather than berating ourselves over our missteps, we can welcome opportunities to learn from those mirrors in life.

As humans with built-in resistance, we often need incentives to move into processing that feels difficult. We like to have reasons and rewards to justify fixing the marriage issues, making a career transition, or changing bad health habits. Regardless of your rationale, entering into your issue with an open mind and an open heart will benefit your life and refine your path forward for your greatest happiness. *You have to go through it, not around it or over it, to get to the prize of transcending it.*

The more resistance you feel to an issue, the more important it is to your spiritual path. If you didn't have what it takes to overcome it, you wouldn't be feeling the resistance in the first place — because your consciousness would avoid the recognition of that issue. Avoidance comes in many forms. Resentment, anger, scorn, nonchalance, and superiority are but a few of its disguises. If you feel any of these, the universe is telling you it's time to get to work.

We can learn the most from people we understand the least. They bring opportunities to learn acceptance, cooperation, humility, compassion, forgiveness, and unconditionality. Through taking in these people and circumstances as mirrors of our own state of consciousness, we uncover depths and make discoveries about ourselves. Our greatest teachers can be those who bring the most conflict, because they present our biggest lessons to overcome. Seemingly minor or random encounters with others matter as well. When we see ourselves more clearly, we can either choose to shift our perspectives and change our lives, or we can remain stagnant. Choosing to avoid, ignore, or project blame at these spiritual junctures keeps us idle and dormant — seemingly safe, but still within a cocoon that shuts out the chance to flourish in our understanding of life. As contemporary music icon Usher says, "Evolve or evaporate."

In each moment of our lives, we engage from where we are. We may not always have the capacity to dig deeply into processing, which may be more or less possible at other times and in other circumstances. There is no shame or guilt in not fulfilling obligations we're not up to. This is why we are here for each other. Mutual support is the backbone of unity. Ultimately, in the bigger picture, we are all working together.

Questions for Reflection

- Identify the mirrors in your life that have shown up as people, circumstances, and physical conditions.

- What do you consider to have been your biggest mistake?

- What are the patterns of conflict that come around again and again for you?

- Name the emotional form your avoidance takes?

- What has been your biggest lesson?

- Who has been your greatest teacher?

NOTES

NOTES

NOTES

NOTES

NOTES

NOTES

NOTES

NOTES

NOTES

NOTES

YOUR UNIQUE FILTER

You are born with infinite potential and infinite paths of purpose, rather than only one pre-chosen path. Your purpose is to explore and expand through the emotional and mental processing of your life. You are born with DNA that has a very unique combination of characteristics that create a filter with which to shape your life. While the circumstances of our lives are not preordained, we attract circumstances that will use the gifts we brought in with us.

Our DNA, combined with what we eat, the environment we live in, the larger culture, how we treat our bodies and minds, and countless other factors, makes up a personal vibrational field that I call a *signature vibration*. Your signature vibration has resonance or dissonance with all that you encounter. You are drawn toward and react to an infinite number of potentials. You're subtly drawn toward or repelled by people, places, and things — whether you're aware of it or not. Along the way, you use your will to discern, choose, process, and experience.

Your ultimate path and potential is embedded within the interactions of these vibrational fields. You are destined to engage in circumstances and with people whose vibrations you resonate with. *But how you assimilate those interactions is up to you.* Love, attraction and passion are the feelings of deep resonance. We can feel passion and attraction to areas of life that are negative as well. In that case, you may be called to ameliorate situations such as poverty or abuse. All these together are your sublime guide to your own greatest purpose.

You are an empowered creator as you live your life. It is up to you how you explore, how far you explore, and how deeply you explore. The universe's exquisite plan is to allow the infinite to find its own way. As the multitude of humans contribute themselves to the whole, the full exploration of humanity takes place. Evolution adapts to us as we adapt to it.

Questions for Reflection

- Who and what have you had the greatest resonance with?

- Who and what have you had the greatest dissonance with?

- What was the lesson in that dissonance?

NOTES

NOTES

NOTES

NOTES

NOTES

NOTES

RAISING VIBRATIONS

Every single hurt or pain we *intentionally* process raises the energetic vibrations of our being and brings us to a better place. Like ripples on a pond, the intentional, conscious clearing of our personal energetic fields helps clear the environment, and ultimately contributes to clearing for the collective. If we process life rather than stuffing our emotions and reactions, our resultant understanding becomes an aspect of collective consciousness, adding to the databank, becoming available for download by every being in the universe. One core purpose of individual processing is to raise the vibrations of all.

SUPRA SEX THROUGH VIBRATIONAL UNION

Barbara Marx Hubbard has coined the concept of *suprasex*. When people are attracted to each other, the universe is uniting them in order to strengthen a higher calling. Where passion for a particular mission is mutual, the impulse gains synergy. This phenomena expands brilliance in all areas of life and promotes the flow of integral evolution.

Likewise, when two people feel that they were meant to be together romantically, they are experiencing this great effect with each other. The resonance of their respective ancestries may be significantly in sync in specific ways, and the trajectories of their mutual fields into the future may be harmoniously concordant as well.

A different type of scenario can occur when opposites attract. In this case, the experiences that one person most needs to learn for the benefit of spiritual maturity are freely available from the field of the other, even if the lessons or understandings are learned through conflict.

All of these potent blueprints of attraction offer the promise of sublime fulfillment that is physically felt through vibrational fields.

The way to your greatest union with another is through allowing your most authentic self to emerge and express. When two purely authentic people come together and resonate, their relationship will be monumentally notable. In a sense, their connection is meant to be. We've heard the legendary tales of pairs who were attuned enough to recognize that resonance in each other. Such an experience is a compelling and meaningful phenomenon for those who've experienced it, and is called forward by a devotion to authenticity.

DEATH AS TEACHER

My mother once observed after a funeral, "Have you noticed that those who were talked about during their lives as being less than kind, perhaps even ruthless, are remembered fondly after they've passed?" We naturally tend to recall good times with people who have passed on. Their positive traits seem to come to mind easier once we know we won't have to endure their negative traits any longer. But it can take time to let go when our experiences of someone included pain. In hindsight, we may suddenly realize what our part was in the struggle with them, and how we might have done things differently. *These insights change us.* We might experience regret and sorrow, but that helps us mature into a greater understanding of what we can do differently the next time we face a similar relationship or situation.

As we mature spiritually, we are able to make changes in our relationships based on what we learned from our past experiences, as well as share with others what we've learned. By processing the grief or lessons around the death of someone we know, we can learn to appreciate the people in our lives in their fully human conditions. We can feel more deeply grateful for the people and circumstances in our present. We may become more accepting of others, of ourselves, and of life itself. *Death can be a great teacher for those who are aware enough to accept its gifts.*

I've also observed that once a person is gone, often someone else will take on their roles and some of their characteristics. People may imitate their parents and mentors after they're gone, often subconsciously. Family members and friends can have this effect on us. In this way, when we die, our thoughts, actions, words, and intentions live on. This is the footprint we leave. Our effect on others reaches profoundly into the future.

When bullies or evil-seeming people die, we often see the larger society begin to make amends, such as through peace movements, educational campaigns, and support for those left behind. This is an inherent rebalancing drive impelled by the evolutionary impulse.

Some people believe in life after death and others do not. Whether or not we live forever, the effects of our engagement with the world in this lifetime does transform the future of humanity. Consciousness stores the essence of you and your thoughts and actions so that they can be accessed by all those who live after you. In the same way, those who came before us, since time immemorial, continue to live on through us — through you, right now. This is why one of our purposes is to hand down our realizations in life.

Questions for Reflection

- What words or actions from someone who has passed on do you recall?

- How have you thought or felt differently about a friend or loved one after they died?

- What words or actions of yours would you like others to remember after you're gone?

NOTES

NOTES

NOTES

NOTES

SERVICE

"We are not put on this earth to see through one another.

We are put on this earth to see one another through."

Gloria Vanderbilt

The path of service is a gratifying journey. When you take a step to serve in the world, you amplify gratification in your being. Sharing yourself with others to assist and support them spreads goodwill far and wide. Serving can take any of a multitude of forms, including assisting physically, cultivating good intentions, and even meditating for balance and peace within yourself.

Engage in the type of service that feels most authentic to your soul. Living and expressing your authenticity by entering into service on behalf of others models how to live with meaning and purpose. But that is not the only way to be of service. Living authentically in and of itself is a great service to the world as well.

AUTHENTICITY AND PURPOSE

Your authentic values in life are exclusive catalysts that drive your original purpose. They are intimate cues to your own greatest potential.

Note that values that are handed down or imposed by people, organizations, or culture may or may not be specifically authentic to you. Although a tribal mentality worked for humanity through certain stages in the growth of our species, the evolutionary impulse now seeks your individually authentic insights, desires, and values. Another way to think of it is that the evolutionary impulse expresses itself through your authentic interpretation. By purging old conditioning and standardized truths, and by growing into spiritual courage and responsibility, your authentic values will emerge. You can use those to create vocationally in ways that are most fulfilling to you. Processing life in this way brings authenticity — and that is your greatest individual purpose.

How we handle the crises and experiences in our lives either aligns or misaligns us with our original authenticity. Relying on guidance from stories that encourage you to hand over your personal responsibility to someone or something else that's inauthentic, or allowing them to do your processing for you, robs you of the opportunity to refine your own spiritual path toward your greatest authenticity.

Though humanity has recognized many people through the ages for their contributions of service, creativity, or leadership, such accolades are not singled out by the universe as notable above the actions of the masses in the forwarding of consciousness. Ego brings the tendency to rate and compare, but all authentic intentions and efforts are significant for the progression of consciousness. Your purpose is to process your way to the most authentic expression of you. This is the greatest contribution you can make.

Questions for Reflection

- How aligned are you with your most authentic self?

- In what specific ways could you come closer?

NOTES

NOTES

NOTES

All of the processing of life we do, every word we speak, every thought we think and every breath we take, is done on behalf of humanity, on behalf of consciousness, on behalf of the universe, and for evolution itself.

As you process your way through your life, let go of all that has outlived its purpose. When you do this, you will lead humanity into a more unencumbered, *unburdened* state of consciousness, helping us all to free ourselves of all that is not serving us any longer.

Sharing the results of your processing expedites our collective growth even further. We learn from each other in this lifetime, through and across eras and dimensions. Even your thoughts that are never shared comprehensively inform collective consciousness. Your decisions ripple forward to change the course of humanity. Your creating influences evolution. You are always on the leading edge, whether you realize it or not. You are significant to the whole beyond comprehension.

Those who live with wholehearted purpose feel the meaning of life in their being. That sense of meaning eliminates floundering and feelings of being ungrounded or unworthy — issues so many of us have faced. We achieve a state of wholehearted purpose by moving authentically through our lives.

Your *individual* purpose is to be your most authentic self. Our *collective* human purpose is to support others on their path. *Universal* purpose materializes as evolution progresses in a self-informing cycle, a united collaboration through time and space. The collective evolutionary intent is to explore, discover, and expand life through time and space.

You are one of the evolutionary impulse's calibration tools.

You, as you truly are, are significantly valuable to life itself.

Be you.

Questions for Reflection

- What theme emerges around purpose in your life?

- Can you identify more than one area of attraction and passion that you have?

NOTES

NOTES

NOTES

NOTES

NOTES

CHAPTER 9

EVOLVING THROUGH SENSES

GAINING EXPANDED PERSPECTIVES

I remember the exciting advent of the Internet during my years of working with small, high-tech startups. In the beginning, it was seen as an adrenaline-pumping timesaver for the Type A, Tony Robbins disciples looking for every possible production advantage for research, document delivery, and efficient communication. The unprecedented explosion of Internet use for commercial as well as personal use brought a paradigm shift to every level of our society. Where females had traditionally been stereotyped to be browsers in the marketplace, now males too were burning the midnight oil with their own version of browsing the world on the Web. We went gaga over technology. Our relationship to life would never be the same.

Simultaneously, the Web allowed more people access to research and discoveries into previously obscure realms of native and metaphysical phenomena. Scores of spiritually minded people could learn about philosophies and practices in the world beyond their community's temples and churches. Interest in indigenous beliefs, ancient knowledge, and quantum research skyrocketed. Professionals in the medical and health fields began to gain a more comprehensive picture of the efficacy of energy work and sensory development. Documentation in these edgy fields became more and more mainstream. Increasing respect for the practices was being realized at all levels of society. Hand-in-hand with the rise of the novel technology of the Internet, the ancient had become new again as well. And for good reason.

THE NEW AGE OF INTUITION

While still in the midst of the Information Age, humans are synchronistically re-entering an Intuition Age — not for the first time, but once again since ancient times. Our species has shifted back into a paradigm of expanded perspectives. Some people are more comfortable with gathering information through digital technology, others lean toward gathering information through scientific exploration. In any case, we also inherently possess a more natural means of gathering information. Our own senses, particularly when developed, give us capabilities to perceive beyond what can be known through traditional methods of testing.

Many high-tech CEOs have been interviewed about how they gained insights for new innovations through their personal meditations. Creative geniuses and artists have traditionally unleashed their senses to experience visions that stretch beyond traditional boundaries. Even Einstein credited his imagination for giving him answers to his universal queries.

At this juncture of humanity, we have the incredible gifts of science and technology while still being able to tap into our natural and authentic connections to the universe as well.

INTEGRAL UNIVERSE

We live in an integral universe. Every part of our world is connected to the whole of information stored in consciousness. Science is verifying that knowledge is not actually stored in specific locations but is non-local. Subatomic particles, such as electrons, have been shown in specific circumstances to instantaneously communicate with each other, whether they are an inch away or thousands of miles apart. This illustrates that knowledge can be known and shared relatively instantaneously.

Throughout human history, discoveries and practices have popped up all over the planet at relatively the same time. Advancements in language and the use of calendars, astronomy, writing, and ships showed up during the same eras on different continents during times when those cultures knew little or nothing about each other. This phenomena occurs because once a discovery, assimilation, or processing has taken place, it is "uploaded" into the collective consciousness, giving humanity access to it for "downloading."

We are connected to the universe at quantum levels. Those who have practiced higher consciousness techniques such as meditation, psychic sensing and channeling understand through experience that one can "open" to knowledge such that a transfer or communication takes place. I have led thousands of people through many types of exercises to demonstrate these phenomena.

We typically live in relatively myopic worlds, mostly aware of only the people, places, and things right in front of us. While we feel emotions and a plethora of thoughts churn around in our minds, we're rarely consciously aware of the volume and diversity of information coming in through our senses at all times. When we transcend the limitations of our physical form, we naturally become engaged with the infinite energy of life. It is highly empowering to practice developing the senses that awaken your own untapped magnitude of consciousness.

BODIES MAKE SENSE

Our original knowledge came from our senses. Animals make use of their senses to navigate their world, and they have not been conditioned out of doing so as we humans have, by believing stories that serve political, cultural, or religious purposes.

You are made as a perfect antennae, tuned to the universe. Your senses give you a foundation for assessing every moment. *Through your senses, you can comprehend patterns and connections to develop an integral picture of the universe that informs you beyond the filter of your beliefs.*

Your organs, and even your skin, provide much information. The well-known phrases "my skin crawled" and "the hairs on my skin stood up" illustrate your senses' messages to you to be cautious, to gauge a person or situation for potential danger. You have also learned much about your world through your heart's reactions to life. The highly respected HeartMath Institute and other organizations are researching the concept that the human heart has its own type of brain. It is not only your *mind* that is connected to universal consciousness.

Our instincts are a fruit of the evolutionary impulse. They override our egos to speak to us. Ego can't always effectively control the scene when it is time for action. Instincts are an innate survival mechanism. Intuition is a step up from instincts on the evolutionary scale. Intuition involves more cognizance than instinct does, but still does not bring full intellect into the mix. Senses inform both instinct and intuition. By paying attention to our senses, we gain more knowledge about the world, including the people around us. More significantly, we learn about ourselves, as in who we are and how our future lives will best be served.

Questions for Reflection

- Reflect on a specific time when your body gave you information about what was happening around you. What were the specifics? Did your stomach churn? Did the hairs on the back of your neck stand up? Did your skin crawl?

- Vividly recall the details of that situation. What messages did your senses attempt to convey to you?

- Did you heed the advice? If not, what was the outcome of not heeding your senses?

NOTES

NOTES

NOTES

SEPARATED FROM OURSELVES

In ancient times, authorities in some societies took jurisdiction of sexual activities, including the individual's private practices. They deemed what was right and what was wrong, including terms that had to do with sexual manner, frequency, and the ages of the participants. For further reinforcement, those edicts were declared to be ordained. As a result, people became separated from their bodies, not having full sovereignty over their own physicality.

Similarly, cultures around the planet have protocols for how emotional expression should be carried out or controlled. For example, the expression of grief was often given free license for one year after the passing of a loved one. Other cultures tend to the griever for one month, or perhaps even only one week. During that time the griever is supported and community members help with cooking and other household tasks. Conversely, the display of anger in public is curtailed by clear social boundaries. Even jealousy is kept to hushed whispers in polite society. Depression is often hidden away behind closed doors.

While these codes of conduct were put into place for well-intentioned reasons, *among the consequences we've experienced is that we became separated from our own bodies, from our emotions and our senses.* These implications are important and far-reaching, as social restrictions have numbed us to an otherwise more authentic basis for operating our lives.

Once cultures acclimated to edicts accepted as being ordained, those who embodied organic extra-sensory perceptions were then thought to be entering areas where only the ordained should be allowed. Sensory engagement was declared dangerous and those who cultivated a broader understanding of their senses were considered to be evil. If the average layperson had been allowed to do what only the ordained had granted themselves the privilege of doing, then there would be no more need for the ordained to provide that role of liaison to the divine within the community. For great segments of the human population, our instincts, intuition, and natural extra-sensory perceptions were further disavowed and consequently buried from our awareness.

MAKING NO SENSE

We are a society of people with dulled down senses. This keeps us from having to face a reality of living in a society of violence, where we experience differences with others in ways our egos haven't learned to harmonize with, and fears that would overwhelm us if we didn't shut them out of our physical experience.

News reports are filled with stories about the masses turning blind eyes to dramatic scenes. If our senses were fully awakened, how could we turn our blind eyes and deaf ears to muggings, racism, and people lying motionless on the street?

From the dramatic to the mundane, we disconnect from that which would make us feel deeply in a way that we're not ready to deal with. It is time to come back to our senses.

Questions for Reflection

- Have you recognized a dullness or nonchalance around something that your mind told you should care about?

- Think of relationships, work tasks, attending to your health — or broader issues such as war, oppression, or widespread diseases — and reflect on where your mind and your heart are in alignment or not in alignment. What do you discover?

NOTES

NOTES

NOTES

NOTES

NOTES

NOTES

MULTIDIMENSIONAL NAVIGATION

You are a universal explorer.

Many scientists believe there are many more dimensions beyond length, width, and depth — dimensions that are invisible to the naked eye but that have a direct effect on the universe. The Superstring Theory holds that there are ten different dimensions, including the possibility of alternate worlds, and the capability of being able to travel backward and forward in time. What if there are countless dimensions — more than we could put a number limit on?

There is empirical evidence of other dimensional activity and engagement. The practice of psychic skills is thought to be a type of advanced dimensional navigation. Humans have been using their psychic senses naturally all along. It makes sense that we would have used every expanded perspective inherently available to us. Logic has inestimable benefit but it can only take us so far. *Our consciousness is capable of perceiving beyond what can be measured scientifically at this time.* The sensory and the psychic are of the natural world. Gradually, the discipline of science will catch up with understanding a wider range of psychic phenomena. In the meantime, discoveries through practice assist us in understanding what direction formal research should take.

For those actively pursuing self-actualization, there are many skills that can be developed. Skills related to energy work, healing techniques, a broad range of sensory development, toning chemistry through meditation, perceiving past and future, multidimensional communication, telepathy — and more — can all be refined. Even governmental agencies are known to train and utilize remote viewers. Every human is born with multidimensional gifts. Some are stronger than others at birth or by default, but all can be cultivated and honed through training.

EXTRASENSORY PERCEPTION

All through recorded history, humans have written about their knowings beyond what they could hear in local proximity or see or touch in three-dimensional form. The Bible is filled with accounts of physical phenomena such as ethereal appearances and voices from non-physical beings that come from other dimensions. Visions and premonitions abounded. Ancient people were richly attuned to their senses and the energy fields around them. It was a way of life that hadn't yet been stigmatized by political and religious interests.

Humans are born with extrasensory capacities. You can perceive multidimensionally through sight with clairvoyance, through hearing with clairaudience, through feeling with clairsentience, and through highly sensitized "knowing" with claircognizance. You even have super senses that can detect smells and tastes psychically — with clairalience and clairgustance! Any of these extrasensory skills can bring a remarkable amount of information about the present, as well as, in some cases, the past and the future.

Aren't we always seeking more data in life? Whether it's about our circumstances at work, in relationships, with personal health, or any other area, knowledge makes us more secure and confident. The more information we have to help us navigate, the easier decisions about life are to make. We enthusiastically read fiction and go to movies that feature superheroes with amped-up powers, but rarely take full advantage of the super powers we embody naturally.

Jean Houston, PhD, a scholar of and researcher in the field of human capacities, is one of the foremost visionary thinkers of our time. She said, "I think what we call the psychic trait is something that is extended through our nervous system as part of our perceptual sensibilities."

Another multidimensional skill, mediumship, which is communication with those who have died, is considered by some to be a sacrilegious engagement to be feared. This is an outdated belief. Recently, mediums from around the world have been demonstrating the great advantages of this type of communication that brings healing and comfort to loved ones. When asked, many people can relay their experiences of feeling that a loved one who has already passed on is near them for support. This may happen during a wedding, a important family celebration or during times of distress or grief. Mediumship practices have been cornerstones for understanding the world spiritually by many native cultures through the ages.

Channeling is a practice that is gaining attention with advanced meditators. This is the art of embodying knowledge or consciousness from another time or place. Leonardo di Vinci, Abraham Lincoln, Thomas Jefferson, Albert Einstein, and even some of the Beatles have spoken about experiencing these phenomena. One of the programs I teach is called Messages from the Evolutionary Impulse. Sessions are conducted by teleconferencing with Internet gatherings of people around the world to share meditations and information about similar work in these fields. In each session, we channel universal vibrations such as love, peace, the evolutionary impulse itself, purpose, justice, gratitude, and much more. Embodying the very essence of these universal vibrations brings extraordinary insights into our lives, and gives a deeper understanding of humanity's trajectory and the world.

Through my teachings of and experiences in the development of highly sensitized perceptions, I've witnessed notable breakthroughs in spiritual areas of students' lives. Progression into attunement of the senses can bring crucial realizations about past patterns that have created stagnation. Sensory development offers fresh insights to life conflicts. *Such gains in universal perception can deconstruct a future that may have been charged with indecision and fear.*

Exploring and developing extrasensory and multidimensional skills leads to discoveries that raise your game to a new level. Spiritual clarity reveals itself. Your life becomes unobstructed as your consciousness is unburdened. This is truly a worthy and purposeful spiritual path of pursuit.

Questions for Reflection

- Can you recall a time when you just knew something, without being informed in any way that seemed obvious?

- Did you ever see something in your mind or in a dream that later came to pass?

- Have you been aware of what someone was thinking and knew what they were going to say before they said it?

- Have you ever felt that someone who had passed away was near you? Did you feel their presence or hear their voice?

NOTES

NOTES

NOTES

SPIRITUAL INTEGRITY

I'd like to make an important note here about intentions around developing psychic skills. Some people want to start developing this skill simply in order to have answers about what will happen in the future shown to them. Precognition is the ability to see into a future dimension. This type of seeing ahead can ignite a passionate journey forward toward a visualized path. But having answers handed to you can leave the work of processing through the issues and circumstances of your life undone if you attempt to leap from A to Z and skip the understanding and lessons that life brings us.

Although practices and skills like psychic "seeing" can provide invaluable guidance, the evolutionary impulse impels us to process input for ourselves, to the level of our capacity at the time. Our physical bodies are vessels for transforming emotions and filtering all we encounter in life. As we do so, we raise the vibrations on the physical plane and clear the collective consciousness for the advancement of our species. My work with individuals and groups includes developing spiritual, extrasensory, and multidimensional skills — from meditation to psychic abilities — while simultaneously developing spiritual responsibility and integrity as well.

BRANCH OUT

The fields of cosmology, metaphysics and spirituality have greatly expanded our understanding of life in recent decades. Consciousness is an established aspect of our existence. Instincts are part of our natural world. Psychic and multidimensional activities are being formally studied by highly regarded organizations and governments on the world stage. Not having labels or measurements for a concept doesn't make it false or unrealistic. That type of thinking is a sophomoric mentality of ages past. But we still have much to learn.

You may have encountered many terms of speech around transcending the local self, such as *human potential movement*, *transpersonal*, and *non-duality*. These refer to expanded states of consciousness that are beyond the scope of this introductory book. As scientific investigation becomes more prolific regarding those fields, and regarding the extrasensory and the multidimensional, more and more discoveries will occur as the future unfolds.

* * *

We can make use of the range of established bodies of knowledge that we've acquired through the ages. But there is not only one answer to any query. There are many other aspects of your human senses as well that are valuable as tools for processing through to your own personalized clarity, values, and authenticity. Sensory awareness at a multitude of levels will be your best guide. The important point in becoming familiar with the existence of these aspects is to understand that extrasensory development makes sense for our collective future. That future always begins now, in each present moment.

Expanded perception is the path to evolving your life consciously. If you desire to know more about this field and to understand yourself and your world better, then begin practicing to develop your extrasensory capacities. This option exists for you. It's about accepting your birthright as a creation of the universe to seek and discover more about your world. Our enhanced abilities will catalyze collective healing in our lives moving forward as well.

Leave the finite behind in your life and open to the infinite.

Questions for Reflection

- Have you ever wished that a loved one could "see" through your eyes? What would they come to know?

- Are you able to look at life through another's eyes? What do you see from that perspective?

- What value would it bring to your life to do this now?

NOTES

NOTES

CHAPTER 10

EVOLVING THROUGH YOU

As an integral player in this world, the evolutionary impulse seeks to live through your unique expression. Unburdening yourself from counterproductive stories will expand your inner vision and uncover your original, intended path. From there, you build a new relationship with your purpose. The intelligence of the infinite has an ultimate plan that includes your most inspired authenticity. Indeed, your singular choices from moment to moment inform the direction of life itself. The universe is mirrored within you as you are mirrored within the universe. Serendipitously, evolving consciousness ardently supports your awakening to the universal perspective of which you are an integral part.

We honor all who have come before us, and all the insights and constructs they put into place. Nonetheless, we don't want to stay bound within that which was useful at one time but now holds us in stagnation in the face of our rapidly progressing spiritual unfoldment. We do, however, honor the timeless principles of love, charity, and compassion. Every step of mankind has brought us to this moment in time. And we must not get stuck here or lost in the shadows. We have come into this world to carry on.

CHANGE

We are change agents, whether we realize it or not. This never means that we must let go of what is precious to us. We can treasure relationships and memories, pets, and even homes for a lifetime. This involves a delicate dance of discernment about what is really serving us as we evolve through the years of our lives.

Do you want to change? The first step is expanding your perspective. Allow yourself to live without a fixed point of reference. Rather than fearing change, reflect on how your life would be if nothing ever changed. Your future wants to speak through you. Let it.

Albert Einstein said, "Life is like riding a bicycle. To keep your balance you must keep moving." Whether or not our peers, family, or the media recognize the old stories we have all been telling ourselves, it takes spiritual courage to release our attachments. No one else can discern what is most aligned for you and your path. It's all up to you.

CHOICE

The ability to make conscious choices is an extraordinary gift, but it's also a primary spiritual responsibility. Take time to realize the implications of this endowment that are all too often overlooked. Be mindful that you always have a choice about which aspects of yourself and the world you identify with at any particular time. The more deeply you know yourself, the clearer your choices about your ultimate path become. As you mature spiritually, you will be able to hold many views and take on many roles at any one time.

Because every choice is a learning experience that will ultimately carry you forward to your greatest self-actualization, you can't go wrong if you comprehend it as such. Fulfillment is yours to make.

YOU ARE ESSENTIAL

Your life is not a series of meaningless moments thrown together. Neither is your life predetermined. You are an infinite vessel of potential. The vast range of possibilities for your life is the greatest gift the universe could give you.

You are entitled to the privilege of making meaning, and realizing that the facets of your world are connected. Stepping into this privilege will make the difference between a meaningless, confusing, and painful life, and a life that is filled with purpose, understanding, and fulfillment.

You are the product of countless desires and acts of love of those who came before you. Feel into this awe-inspiring bestowal. You are the miracle you seek. You *are* the leading edge of humanity.

Our world needs *you*.

ENLIGHTENMENT

Enlightenment is being in the flow of life. It's about the seeking itself because our capacity to perceive reality is always evolving, and so our comprehension matures along with the progressing unfoldment. We are only ever as enlightened as our next question.

Enlightenment is open-mindedness. Coming to only one conclusion is an attempt to make the infinite finite. However, drawing only one conclusion can be a useful tool for gauging, measuring, and extrapolating — as long as it is only a tool and not the final reference point. Otherwise righteousness will dictate at the very least, a stagnation of consciousness and at the most, a social path of danger and destruction, since morals and virtues vary according to the eye of the beholder. In other words, there is some truth in all things, but no complete truth in any one thing. You really can live comfortably in a state of potential, exploring possibilities, without having *the* answer figured out.

Do you know anyone who achieved their ultimate goal only to become depressed and uninspired afterward? That happens because we aren't meant to rest in an arbitrary state of achievement forever. Triumph crowns the ego's crest, but there will always be a higher point to be sought further on.

Without this human drive for progress, we might still be sporting fur coats that are attached to our skin! This isn't to say that we should perpetually knock ourselves out to attain more, without rest or reflection. Our achievements are exciting and gratifying and we can be proud of them. It is fulfilling and fruitful to rest in place and assimilate what we've gained. The point is to remember that there is, and will always be, a bigger and deeper picture at hand.

Those who know me best will tell you that my usual observation at any given time is, "This is where I am now. Who knows what I'll think in the future?" Only inquiry will lead us to the next piece of the puzzle, as all things are contained in the flow.

Because, with the broadest point of view, all things are relevant, we can now take an inclusive perspective. Further, *a deep mending of the spirit* comes when we can include more of life's perspectives in our awareness. Embrace every change, perspective and step, as you travel along your way.

Your life is right now, happening from within you. It is not out there or back then or one day in the future. Step into recognizing your passion, feeling your passion, and being your passion. Allow yourself to experience the raw, tender, and beautiful human parts of you. *They are valuable to the entire world.*

As we face ourselves, we heal humanity.

Embrace life. Embrace yourself.

LIVING CONSCIOUSLY

What if life is what we make of it? What if our personal

processing furthers the whole shebang along? What if your purpose is to be yourself?

The old paradigm of asking for your purpose to be divinely revealed is backwards. We determine our purpose through making choices and taking actions with the divinely inspired consciousness we are born with. We empower the grand design by using what it has given us inherently.

We have meaning to make and purpose to realize. It's in the details of everyday life that the most profound spiritual revelations may be found.

Each moment can bring you to an understanding of who you are and why you're here. Stay open to the people, places, words, and acts that you encounter. Your spiritual growth is waiting in the hidden places and the hardest lessons. It is also to be found in the warmest embraces and in laughter and love. Living consciously will bring expanded capacities and more profound meaning to your life.

* * *

Evolution can't not happen. So, how will you evolve?

We are positioned at the inception of a new consciousness, with the potential for more awareness and more global connection than ever before.

The evolutionary impulse realizes itself through you. You are on the threshold of your own personal inner revolution, if you choose. Transformation takes place with every thought and every breath, moving the collective flow forward. Your own personal self-actualization occurs in the same way. Immersing in the universal flow releases stagnation and suffering, if only we allow it.

Knowledge is a byproduct of enlightened exploration, but reverence for life itself — for one another and for the Earth that supports us — is the inspiration for our seeking. When we give love, we nourish humanity. When we spread acceptance and compassion in the world, we heal humanity. We move the world forward.

You move the world forward.

"We must go rejoicing in the blessings of this world... chief of which is the mystery, the magic, the majesty and the miracle that is life."

Wyatt Emory Cooper (Anderson Cooper's father)

May you cultivate a passion to know your most authentic self. May you be responsible for who you are and courageous in your choices. May you honor the purpose you bring to the world. And may you be inspired to see your life anew.

Life celebrates you.

Thank you for being here.

ADDITIONAL QUESTIONS FOR REFLECTION

- How might you consciously participate in relationships in order to bring more harmony to your interactions with others? List as many as you can.

- What is one of your fears that is based in old stories and that could be let go of?

- How might it feel if you completely let go of insecurity for the rest of your life?

- How might it feel if you completely let go of judgment of yourself and others for the rest of your life?

- How willing are you to let go of insecurity and judgment?

- What is your capacity for creativity?

- What is your capacity for love?

- What is your capacity for joy and fulfillment?

- Are you in alignment with what you want to bring to the world?

- What is the best-case scenario that could result from a change in your perspective of your life?

- If nothing ever evolved from where you are today in your life, what would you miss out on?

- If you could come back and do your life again, what would you do differently?

- What do you want your legacy to be?

NOTES

NOTES

NOTES

NOTES

NOTES

NOTES

NOTES

NOTES

NOTES

NOTES

NOTES

NOTES

NOTES

ACKNOWLEDGMENTS

I want to acknowledge and thank Mark Julian, my confidant, kindred journey mate, and spiritual consort who was the catalyst for this book to come into being when it did. After many months of long, cozy dates curled up together with our laptops through snow, spring blossoms, mosquitoes, and fall foliage, here we are! I am as excited about him publishing his book as I am about mine. It's been fun and funny and rich and poignant and warm and fulfilling to immerse in this whole process side by side with him. I don't know that I could write again without the constant supply of vivacious flowers by my side that he's kept me supplied with. His support is priceless to me and I look forward to much more ahead. This is only the beginning...

Thanks to Wendy Leon, my dear friend and long-time private student — I can't thank her enough for her generous support in getting this book started. I'm mystified by concepts of organization, so her setting up a system and cataloguing tens of thousands of words from such a kaleidoscope of broad and enigmatic notes was exactly the foundation I needed to catapult me into the world of writing a book. I won't forget her encouragement, which started years before the writing did! I hold heartfelt gratitude for her, and encourage her to keep on keeping on with her own important work in the world.

Thanks to Grace Kerina, my chief editor, who I am convinced was born to edit. What a mind she has for the written word!

I have never known anyone who could find the most perfect words within a split second the way she can. Wow. I have so appreciated her throughout this entire process! Yes, Grace, you have my permission to edit this paragraph. (I wouldn't dare! — Grace)

I also want to acknowledge all the very special individuals I've been fortunate enough to work with over the years. I especially recognize my long-term students: Nicki Green, Amber Miller, Kathy Beach, Carla Grillo, Jessica F., and Melissa Fundanish, who have given me memories to last a lifetime. I celebrate other clients and students who have lent invaluable experiences along the way: Rena Huisman, Dr. Joshua Kai, Thomas Workman Ph.D., Pat Ulrich, Janie Daum, Kitty Monroe, Lois Beach, Jackie Brucker, and many others, all of whom have a place in my heart. I learned and gained so much from their openness and willingness to engage wholeheartedly. I'm grateful for their trust in me and for recognizing life's impulse in me to carry on this work. I honor the same in each of them.

And thanks to you, dear reader, for being open to considering expanded perspectives on all that you've known in your life. As you do so, you open the door for humanity to do the same.

ABOUT THE AUTHOR

Sheila Cash is an international teacher, spiritual mentor, author, speaker, and facilitator in the fields of human potential and conscious evolution. She has founded numerous progressive groups on the development of universal perspectives and expanding sensory capacities. Using an integrated blend of ancient and contemporary modalities from science, psychology and philosophy, she guides clients into innovative inquiry and practical exploration into life's mysteries.

Sheila coaches groups and individuals to explore and see how all parts of their lives fit seamlessly into the conscious universe. A visionary and original thinker, she helps people put the puzzle pieces of their life together and relate it the bigger picture: why we are here, what our purpose is, and what life is really all about. Connecting equally with her students' minds and hearts, her teachings transcend standard how-to instructions and self-help manuals to awaken a deeper understanding of how our collective evolutionary path can bring genuine alignment to our individual lives.

Sheila redefines spirituality in a comprehensive and integral way for the people she works with. In the unfolding of deeper truths, a new understanding of reality is synthesized, illuminating authenticity and purpose in the process.

Sheila navigates with unconditional acceptance and sees the humanity in all those she encounters. She delights in the increasing unfoldment of our global community, and in the connections with people she makes every day.

www.sheilacash.com

www.evolveyourlife.org

THANK YOU

Dear Reader, it is the end of this book but the beginning of your journey forward from here. Are you ready to continue your expansion of discovery?

Let's keep talking!

To support you, I invite you to pick up a voucher code for **$100 off** of the upcoming comprehensive online course series that follows from this book where readers connect and explore more deeply with others. We value your unique insights!

And don't forget to find your **"Daily Evolutionary Sparks" ~ short bursts of revelatory wisdom on your evolutionary path forward!** Choose to take a peek, or have them delivered directly to you!

To find out more about the community, the online series, the *Daily Evolutionary Sparks* and to get the voucher code, visit www.sheilacash.com/book-thanks, or www.evolveyourlife.org

I wish you a profound journey as you move forward in your life. Stay in touch!

difference press

Difference Press offers entrepreneurs, including life coaches, healers, consultants, and community leaders, a comprehensive solution to get their books written, published, and promoted. A boutique-style alternative to self-publishing, Difference Press boasts a fair and easy-to-understand profit structure, low-priced author copies, and author-friendly contract terms. Its founder, Dr. Angela Lauria, has been bringing to life the literary ventures of hundreds of authors-in-transformation since 1994.

LET'S MAKE A DIFFERENCE WITH YOUR BOOK

You've seen other people make a difference with a book. Now it's your turn. If you are ready to stop watching and start taking massive action, reach out.

"Yes, I'm ready!"

In a market where hundreds of thousands books are published every year and are never heard from again, all participants of The Author Incubator have bestsellers that are actively changing lives and making a difference.

In two years we've created over 134 bestselling books in a row, 90% from first-time authors. We do this by selecting the highest quality and highest potential applicants for our future programs.

Our program doesn't just teach you how to write a book—our team of coaches, developmental editors, copy editors, art directors, and marketing experts incubate you from book idea to published bestseller, ensuring that the book you create can actually make a difference in the world. Then we give you the training you need to use your book to make the difference you want to make in the world, or to create a business out of serving your readers. If you have life-or world-changing ideas or services, a servant's heart, and the willingness to do what it REALLY takes to make a difference in the world with your book, go to http://theauthorincubator.com/apply/ to complete an application for the program today.

OTHER BOOKS BY DIFFERENCE PRESS

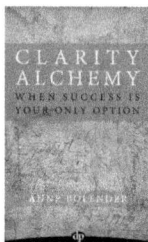

Clarity Alchemy:
When Success Is
Your Only Option

by Ann Bolender

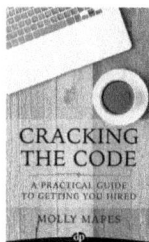

Cracking the Code:
A Practical Guide
to Getting You
Hired

by Molly Mapes

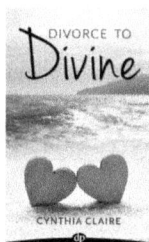

Divorce to Divine:
Becoming the
Fabulous Person
You Were Intended
to Be

by Cynthia Claire

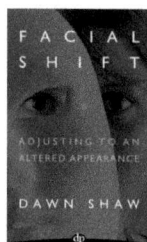

Facial Shift:
Adjusting to an
Altered Appearance

by Dawn Shaw

Finding Clarity:
Design a Business
You Love and
Simplify Your
Marketing

by Amanda H.
Young

Flourish: Have
It All Without
Losing Yourself

by Dr. Rachel Talton

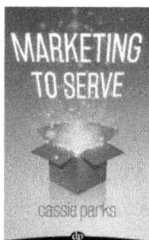

Marketing
To Serve: The
Entrepreneur's
Guide to Marketing
to Your Ideal
Client and Making
Money with Heart
and Authenticity

by Cassie Parks

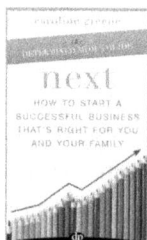

NEXT: How to
Start a Successful
Business That's
Right for You and
Your Family

by Caroline Greene

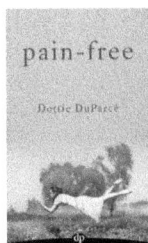

*Pain Free: How I
Released 43 Years
of Chronic Pain*

by Dottie DuParcé
(Author), John F.
Barnes (Foreword)

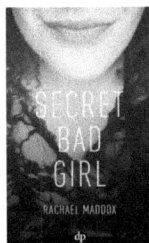

*Secret Bad Girl:
A Sexual Trauma
Memoir and
Resolution Guide*

by Rachael
Maddox

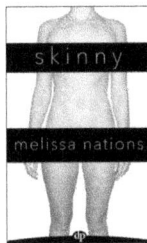

*Skinny: The Teen
Girl's Guide to
Making Choices,
Getting the Thin
Body You Want,
and Having the
Confidence You've
Always Dreamed Of*

by Melissa Nations

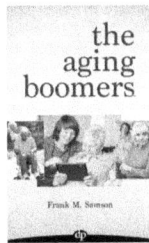

*The Aging Boomers:
Answers to Critical
Questions for You,
Your Parents and
Loved Ones*

by Frank M. Samson

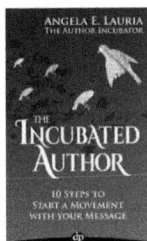

*The Incubated
Author: 10 Steps to
Start a Movement
with Your Message*

by Angela Lauria

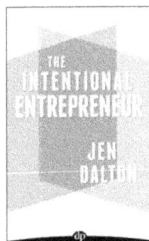

*The Intentional
Entrepreneur: How
to Be a Noisebreaker,
Not a Noisemaker*

by Jen Dalton
(Author), Jeanine
Warisse Turner
(Foreword)

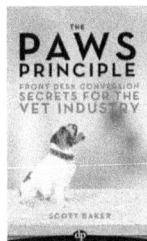

*The Paws Principle:
Front Desk
Conversion Secrets
for the Vet Industry*

by Scott Baker

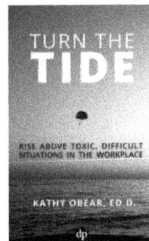

*Turn the Tide:
Rise Above Toxic,
Difficult Situations
in the Workplace*

by Kathy Obear